FINE COTTON PAPERS

BLUE BOOK

STATIONERY

THE STYLES AND ETIQUETTE OF LETTERS, NOTES, AND INVITATIONS

Edited by Steven L. Feinberg

CRANE & CO., INC.
Dalton, Massachusetts

*Common sense and consideration should be the
basis of etiquette and good manners.*
— John Quincy Adams

Crane's Blue Book of Stationery: The Styles and Etiquette of Letters
Notes, and Invitations/Edited by Steven L. Feinberg - 2nd ed.

Published by Crane & Co., Inc.
30 South Street
Dalton, MA 01226

ISBN 0-9722921-0-1

Printed in the United States of America

FOREWORD

*I*n the midst of this fast-paced and often impersonal world of digital technology where messages disappear almost as soon as they are delivered, the arrival in your mailbox of a finely engraved invitation or a personal note on elegant, timeless stationery has greater impact than ever before.

We at Crane's are honored that, for more than 200 years, you have selected our papers to chronicle so many of life's important events, whether that's a congratulatory note for a promotion, the announcement of a new baby, an invitation to a family wedding or a simple heart-felt thank you. Seven generations of our family, and as many generations of our employees, continue to carry on the heritage our ancestors began in 1801 — to make the finest 100% cotton papers in the world.

We are pleased to bring you our Blue Book of Stationery, which contains time-tested styles and etiquette for letters, notes, and invitations. It is the legacy of many generations of social and professional correspondence covering a wide range of occasions, some quite common, others less familiar.

We hope these pages will serve not as hard and fast rules of social conduct, but as guidelines to help you navigate a variety of occasions where personal correspondence is an important element — an enduring document to make the events of a lifetime more memorable and meaningful for generations to come.

Lansing Crane

CONTENTS

CONTENTS

CONTENTS

CONTENTS

THE ESSENCE OF ETIQUETTE

*E*tiquette can be defined as the body of rules of social conduct that tells us what our society considers appropriate and acceptable behavior. Adherence to these guidelines can help make our personal and professional relationships more comfortable and effective. We tend to feel more at ease when we understand what others expect of us.

The etiquette that we follow when sending a letter or invitation, like etiquette in other areas, revolves around three basic building blocks: Common sense, courtesy, and usage.

Etiquette's foundation is common sense. On an invitation, for example, there is essential information that must be conveyed if you want your guests to show up at your event. Your guests need to know who is inviting them to what function. They also need to know the date, time, and place. A properly worded invitation contains all of that information and presents it succinctly and coherently.

Courtesy is the spirit of etiquette. Its inherent generosity makes for better and more rewarding relationships. Courtesy imposes on us an obligation to be considerate of others. While using this book, you may come across some guidelines that you feel might not work in your situation. If you followed those guidelines, you might, perhaps, offend someone you love. You may feel that your relationship with that person is more important than the wording of your invitation. When that is the case, courtesy demands that you find an alternative. Etiquette is proper only when it facilitates and strengthens relationships.

The third building block is usage. Etiquette has evolved over the years and will continue to evolve. Many of the customs that were proper fifty years ago are anachronisms now - a gentleman tipping his hat comes to mind. Likewise, many of the customs we practice today will be outdated fifty years from now.

As old customs become obsolete, new ones take their place. Reply cards, for example, were, not very long ago, considered improper, even offensive and insulting. Wedding invitations were always answered in one's own handwriting on one's own stationery. As our lives became busier and busier, many of us no longer had the time to sit down and handwrite a reply. Since hosts and hostesses could not risk not receiving responses, they began to send reply cards with their invitations. This made it easier for their guests to respond. The courtesy extended to their guests was a common sense approach to the problem of late and never received responses. As more and more invitations were sent with reply cards, reply cards became more and more acceptable. Today, they are sent with almost every wedding invitation.

In other words, at some point the traditional way of responding to wedding invitations was not working. Common sense suggested that a solution be developed. The solution was simple: Extend to guests the courtesy of providing them with an easy to use card with a stamped, pre-addressed envelope. This solution worked and through its usage reply cards have now become perfectly proper.

These three building blocks - common sense, courtesy, and usage - are the basis for all the guidelines that social etiquette provides.

SOCIAL
STATIONERY

YOUR SOCIAL STATIONERY WARDROBE

*A*s with the clothes you wear, the stationery you use makes a statement about you. When you create and assemble a stationery wardrobe, it will be helpful to keep in mind the impression you hope to make. Your stationery should reflect both your personality and the type of correspondence that you are sending.

Creating a stationery wardrobe requires asking yourself three important questions:

1. What kind of paper should I use?
2. What should I have printed on my stationery?
3. Should my stationery be printed or engraved?

The remainder of this chapter will attempt to answer those questions and help you select the stationery wardrobe that is most appropriate for you.

WHAT KIND OF PAPER SHOULD I USE?

This is actually a three-part question, as you need to choose the material from which the paper is made, the color, and the types of stationery.

Paper is made from either cotton or wood. The first true papers were made from cotton almost two thousand years ago. Wood-pulp papers came into being in the 1800s during the Industrial Revolution. They supplanted cotton-fiber papers for many uses because of their lower cost and the seemingly endless supply of trees.

The finest paper, though, is made from cotton. Before you order your stationery, run your fingers across the paper. Stationery made from cotton will have a soft, rich feel. You will undoubtedly recognize the quality inherent in cotton-fiber papers. Crane's 100% cotton fiber papers have the touch and feel of uncommonly beautiful papers.

Stationery comes in many different colors. Ecru, also known as buff, cream, and ivory, and white are the most popular but grey, blue, pink, yellow, and other colors are also available.

You can order several different types of stationery. The two most basic are one for writing notes and one for writing longer letters. While these two items are essential, you may wish to add variations of these two as you build your stationery wardrobe. We will discuss different types of stationery in detail later in this chapter.

WHAT SHOULD I HAVE PRINTED ON MY STATIONERY?

How you personalize your stationery depends on the purpose for which the stationery will be used and on what is aesthetically pleasing to you. Your stationery may display your name, your name and address, just your address, your monogram, or even your family crest.

Below are displayed a number of different lettering and monogram styles.

Renée Hendricks Smith

MARTINA ALVAREZ
284 CORDOVA COURT
SAN DIEGO, CALIFORNIA 92107

34 East 82nd Street
New York, New York 10022

SHOULD MY STATIONERY BE PRINTED OR ENGRAVED?

Stationery can be engraved, blind-embossed, thermographed, or flat-printed.

Engraving is one of the oldest and most beautiful processes for reproducing images on paper. The appeal of engraving lies in the exquisite detail created by its three-dimensional impression. Engraving is produced when the copy is etched in reverse into a copper plate. Ink is deposited in the resulting cavity. The engraving press then forces the paper into the cavity, creating a raised impression. The paper is literally raised with the ink adhering to the raised surface. The fact that the paper is raised is what distinguishes engraving from thermography and flat-printing.

Blind-embossing is the same process as engraving minus the ink. The image is simply the raised paper. You might recognize blind-embossing as the raised address on the flap of a wedding envelope.

It is easy to tell whether or not a piece of stationery is engraved. Simply turn it over. If there is an indentation (caused by the pressure from the engraving press), it is engraved. You can also tell by looking closely at the impression on the front. The paper will be smoother there and there may be a little ripple to the sheet. This is called the "bruise" and is a natural part of the process.

Engraved stationery is more expensive than thermographed or flat-printed stationery. However, much of the price difference lies in the initial cost of the engraving plate. Since engraving plates can be used over and over again, subsequent orders of engraved stationery will cost only a little more than other types of stationery.

Thermography is sometimes called "raised printing," although the printing is not raised at all. Unlike engraving where the paper is actually raised, the raise in thermography is created by a resinous powder that is melted over the flat-printed ink. Thermography is less expensive than engraving but, while quite handsome, is not quite as appealing.

Flat-printing, as its name implies, is simply ink applied to a flat surface with no raise.

SOCIAL PAPERS FOR WOMEN

For Letter Writing

Letter Sheets:

Letter sheets, sometimes referred to as "formal stationery", are the most formal papers in a woman's stationery wardrobe. They are ecru or white and have a fold along the left-hand side. (Formal wedding invitations are engraved on letter sheets.) Letter sheets fold again from top to bottom to fit inside an envelope that is approximately half their size.

Blank, unadorned letter sheets are used to reply to formal invitations and for letters of condolence. Because of their simple elegance, letter sheets may be used for any type of correspondence. Letter sheets may be adorned with a coat of arms, a monogram, a name, an address, or simply left blank.

You start your letter on the front page of the letter sheet, followed by page 3. Neither page 2 nor page 4 are written on as one never writes on the back of a sheet of paper. On letter sheets, however, some women prefer to start their letters on page 1. Then they open up the letter sheet, turn it sideways and write lengthwise across pages 2 and 3.

Correspondence Sheets:

Correspondence sheets are single sheets of stationery that fold in half to fit their envelopes. They were once called "half sheets" because they were half the size of formal letter sheets. They may be embellished with your monogram, name, address, or name and address.

Only the front of a correspondence sheet is written on, never the back. If you need additional space, use blank second sheets.

Monarch Sheets:

Monarch sheets, also known as "executive stationery", are used for longer personal letters and for personal business letters. Monarch sheets measure 7 1/4" x 10 1/2" and fold into thirds to fit their envelopes.

A name, address, or name and address appear at the top of the sheet.

Only the front of the sheet is written on, never the back. If you need additional space, use blank second sheets.

For Note Writing

Fold-over Notes:

Fold-over notes are used to write thank-you notes, extend informal invitations, and to send short messages to friends and acquaintances. Your monogram or your name may appear on the notes. The monogram or lettering style that will work best for you is the one that best reflects your personality.

Fold-over notes may begin on page 1 when the imprint is at the top of the note. The note may continue on page 3. When the imprint is in the center of the note, the entire message is written on page 3. Pages 2 and 4 are not used. If you need more space, use a different type of stationery, perhaps a correspondence sheet.

Monograms:

Married women use the initials that represent their first name, maiden name, and married name. When all of the letters in the monogram are the same size, the initials appear in order. If you choose a monogram that has a larger center initial, the initial representing your surname appears in the middle flanked by the initials of your given name on the left and your maiden name on the right.

Single women and married women who retain their maiden name use the initials representing their first, middle, and last names. They appear in order in monograms in which all of the letters are the same size. When using a monogram in which the middle initial is larger, the initial representing the surname appears in the middle, flanked by the initials of the given names.

Names:

Married women use their first name, maiden name, and married name. Single women and women who retain the use of their maiden name use their first, middle, and last names.

Informals:

Contrary to their name, informals are rather formal. Informals are small white or ecru fold-over notes. They are engraved in black ink and may have a panelled frame.

Informals are engraved with a woman's proper social name, preceded by her title. "Mr. & Mrs." is properly used on informals only when they are used to issue an informal invitation from both husband and wife.

Informals are used to issue formal invitations, to send very brief messages, and as gift enclosures. They are not properly used as calling cards or thank-you notes.

You would usually write only on page 3.

Correspondence Cards:

One of the most useful items in a stationery wardrobe is the correspondence card. Less formal than a note, these increasingly popular items, are used for thank-yous, informal invitations, and short notes.

Correspondence cards are flat, heavy cards usually measuring 4 1/4" x 6 1/2" that are mailed in matching envelopes. They can be plain or bordered, depending on one's tastes. A name or a small monogram may appear at the top of the card.

Only the front of the card is written on, never the back. If you need more space, use a different type of stationery, perhaps a correspondence sheet.

House Stationery:

House stationery may be properly used by any resident of your house or by any guest staying at your house. Many people keep house stationery at their country and beach homes so that stationery is always available for their guests and for themselves.

Only the name of your house or your address appears on the stationery.

SOCIAL PAPERS FOR MEN

For Letter Writing

Monarch Sheets:

Most men use monarch sheets for their personal letters and personal business letters. Monarch sheets, also known as "executive stationery", measure 7 1/4" x 10 1/2" and fold into thirds to fit their envelopes. Although monarch sheets are available in a variety of colors, most men prefer ecru or white. Many different ink colors are also available, but most men choose black, grey, or navy blue.

You may display your name, address, or name and address at the top of the sheets. The stationery retains a more personal look when you use only your name.

Only the front of the sheet is written on, never the back. If you need additional space, use blank second sheets.

MATTHEW BARRETT WALKER

Correspondence Sheets:

Men who usually do not write long letters may prefer correspondence sheets to monarch sheets. Measuring 6 1/4" x 8 1/2", correspondence sheets are somewhat smaller than monarch sheets and fold in half to fit their envelopes. They may be embellished with your coat of arms, monogram, or with your name and address. Most men, however, prefer to show just their names.

Like monarch sheets, only the front of a correspondence sheet is written on, never the back. If you need additional space, use blank second sheets.

For Note Writing

Correspondence Cards:

Correspondence cards are small, usually 4 1/4" x 6 1/2", heavy, flat cards that are used for thank-you notes and other brief notes. Men generally use these in lieu of fold-over notes. The cards are very practical and most men find that they use many more correspondence cards than sheets.

Your name or small monogram appears at the top. Some men have their name and address printed across the top of the card.

Only the front of the card is written on, never the back. If you need more space, use a monarch or correspondence sheet instead.

Envelopes:

Envelopes for social stationery are printed with your address on the back flap. Your name can be included, but is usually omitted. If you live in an apartment building, be sure to include the apartment number. The nine digit zip code, normally used in business, may also be used on personal stationery.

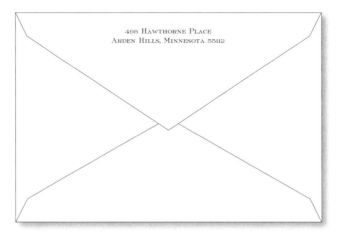

498 Hawthorne Place
Arden Hills, Minnesota 55112

Postcards:

Postcards are used for short, non-confidential correspondence. They are great for reminding people of "that" meeting. They can be printed with either your name or your name and address on one line at the top of the card. The maximum size that the Postal Service allows for reduced rate postage is 4 1/4" x 6".

BUSINESS

AND

PROFESSIONAL

STATIONERY

*E*ach letter written on business stationery is a personal emissary from one office to another. Corporate stationery influences the impression formed in the mind of the recipient, not only about the individual sender, but also about the company they represent.

Several decisions need to be made when creating business and professional stationery:

1. What kind of paper should I use?
2. What items should I include in my corporate stationery wardrobe?
3. What information should I include?
4. What color ink should I use?
5. Should my stationery be engraved, thermographed, or flat-printed?

WHAT KIND OF PAPER SHOULD I USE?

Paper is made from either cotton or wood. The first true papers were made from cotton almost two thousand years ago. Wood-pulp papers came into being in the 1800's during the Industrial Revolution. They supplanted cotton-fiber papers for many uses because of their lower cost and because of the seemingly endless supply of trees.

The finest papers are made from cotton. Before you select your business stationery, run your fingers across the paper. Stationery made from cotton will have a soft, rich feel, just like that of a cotton shirt. It will also be stronger and longer lasting than ordinary papers made from wood or from a combination of cotton and wood. Cotton fiber papers are stronger because the fibers intertwine and adhere to one another. They last longer because cotton fibers are broken down into a pulp by gentle beating as opposed to the harsh acids used to break wood into a pulp. Crane's 100% cotton fiber papers have the touch and feel of uncommonly beautiful papers.

Business papers come in a variety of colors. While ecru (also known as ivory, buff, or cream) and white are the most popular, colors such as grey and blue are frequently used as well.

WHAT COLOR INK SHOULD I USE?

While most businesses choose conservative colors, such as black and grey, more and more businesses are using livelier colors like blue, red, green, gold, bronze, silver, and combinations of two or more of these colors. The correct colors for your business are the ones that best reflect your company and the type of business that you are in.

WHAT ITEMS SHOULD I INCLUDE IN MY CORPORATE STATIONERY WARDROBE?

There are many types of stationery that you might wish to include in your corporate stationery wardrobe. These items range from the basics, such as your corporate letterhead and business cards, to the more personal, such as correspondence cards and jotter cards. Many professionals start with the basics and add other items as their business grows or as their needs increase. This chapter discusses the many items that can make up a professional's stationery wardrobe.

SHOULD MY STATIONERY BE ENGRAVED, THERMOGRAPHED, OR FLAT-PRINTED?

Business and professional stationery can be engraved, thermographed, or flat-printed.

Engraving is one of the oldest and most beautiful processes for reproducing images on paper. The appeal of engraving lies in the exquisite detail created by its three-dimensional impression. Engraving is produced when the copy is etched in reverse into a copper plate. Ink is deposited in the resulting cavity. The engraving press then forces the paper into the cavity, creating a raised impression. The paper is literally raised with the ink adhering to the raised surface. The fact that the paper is raised is what distinguishes engraving from thermography and flat-printing.

It is easy to tell whether or not a piece of stationery is engraved. Simply turn it over. If there is an indentation (caused by the pressure from the engraving press), it is engraved. You can also tell by looking closely at the impression on the front. The paper will be smoother there and there may be a little ripple to the sheet. This is called the "bruise" and is a natural part of the process.

Engraved stationery is more expensive than thermographed or printed stationery. However, much of the price difference lies in the initial cost of the engraving plate. Since engraving plates can be used over and over again, and since business stationery is often run in large quantities, the cost of engraved stationery is not necessarily much more expensive than thermographed or flat-printed stationery.

Thermography is sometimes called "raised printing," although the printing is not raised at all. Unlike engraving where the paper is actually raised, the raise in thermography is created by a resinous powder that is melted over the flat-printed ink. Thermography is less expensive than engraving but, while quite handsome, is not quite as appealing. Since it is less expensive, it might be chosen when smaller quantities are ordered, especially now that laser-friendly inks are available.

Flat-printing, as its name implies, is simply ink applied to a flat surface with no raise.

WHAT INFORMATION SHOULD I INCLUDE?

In the not too distant past, it was fairly easy to decide what information to include on business and professional stationery. You included your company's name, address, phone number, and, perhaps, your name and title. In addition to that information, it now may be necessary to add your fax number, E-mail address, web site, cell phone number, and pager number.

Corporate Letterhead:

This 8 1/2" x 11" sheet is the basic stationery used by most businesses. It is used not only to communicate, but also to project a corporate image. Information on the letterhead may include the firm's name, address, phone number, fax number, and web site. It may also include an executive or partner's name, title, E-mail address, cell phone number, and pager number. Because there can be so much information on the letterhead, many companies are placing some of the information on a line running across the bottom of the page.

M

MEDIA MARKETING

2912 WESTMORELAND AVENUE   DALLAS, TEXAS 75237
214 555 1212

WWW.MEDIA.COM

Most members of a firm use the universal letterhead displaying the corporate identity and the basic information, such as the address and phone number. Partners and senior executives, however, generally use the same letterhead with their name, title and, perhaps, other pertinent information added.

The company name and address appears in the top left corner of the front of the envelope or, less frequently, on the back flap.

RENAUD & LINSCOTT CONSULTANTS
Executive Search and Placement
10 GREENOUGH STREET
CAMBRIDGE, MASSACHUSETTS 02139

PAUL J. RENAUD
PRESIDENT

(617) 555-1212

RENAUD & LINSCOTT CONSULTANTS
Executive Search and Placement
10 GREENOUGH STREET
CAMBRIDGE, MASSACHUSETTS 02139

Monarch Sheets:

Monarch sheets or executive stationery (7 1/4" x 10 1/2") are slightly smaller and, therefore, more personal than the standard 8 1/2" x 11" sheets. Monarch sheets can be used as business letterhead or for personal business letters. They can be used as letterhead in businesses where a personal touch might be helpful, perhaps by designers, consultants, or by executives of small businesses. When used as letterhead, they display the same information found on a standard 8 1/2" x 11" sheet. Since monarch sheets are smaller, you might want to include only essential information.

WOODMAN & TAYLOR REALTY

3584 WESTWOODS ROAD
WHEAT RIDGE, COLORADO 80033
TEL/FAX 303 555 1212

ROBERT J. WOODMAN
CRS, GRI

Personal business letters, mentioned in the last paragraph, are letters sent on behalf of the business to an individual with whom you are on a first name basis. They display only the executive's name at the top of the sheet. The company name and address appears on the back flap of the envelope.

Correspondence Cards:

Many business occasions and meetings call for a brief, personal note as a follow-up, or, perhaps, a congratulatory note needs to be sent. Correspondence cards are the perfect tool to meet these needs. They are flat, heavy cards (4 1/4" x 6 1/4") that are used to send brief notes. The notes are handwritten, letting the recipient know that you cared enough to take the time to write a personal note.

Your name is engraved at the top of your correspondence cards. Your company's name and address appears on the back flap of the envelope.

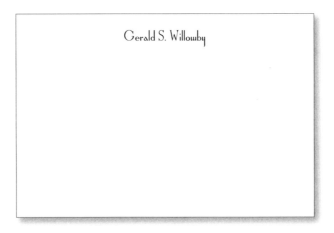

Business Cards:

Business cards provide clients or potential clients with a means of contacting you. They should contain all pertinent information neatly and concisely and be as free from clutter as possible. Remember, they are a communication tool, not an advertisement. Information can include the company name, your name and title, as well as the company's address, phone number, fax number, and web site. While the standard size for a business card, 3 1/2" x 2" is still the most popular, many executives, in order to accommodate so much information, now opt for larger 3 3/8" x 2 1/2" cards or fold-over cards with company name printed on the front.

Most business cards are white or ecru and are printed in black or grey ink but many cards are now being printed on grey or blue stock in various colors, such as red, green, blue, and combinations of two colors to reflect a company's identity.

Green&Hart

Mark H. Richardson
Associate

Green&Hart Investment Group
65 Financial Place
New York, NY 10005
Telephone 212 555-1212
Facsimile 212 555-2121
richardson@greenhart.com

Andrea Haughton
INTERIOR DESIGN

2894 MONTAGUE PLACE
CROTON-ON-HUDSON, NY 10520

914 555 1212

NETWORKS

NICK LOWE
EXECUTIVE VICE PRESIDENT
STRATEGIC DEVELOPMENT

1801 POST ROAD
WESTPORT, CONNECTICUT 06880
TEL: 203.555.1212   FAX: 203.555.2121

ONE STATE STREET PLAZA
SAN FRANCISCO, CALIFORNIA 94107
TEL: 415.555.1212   FAX: 415.555.2121

E-MAIL: NLOWE@NETWORKS.COM

Social Business Cards:

Business cards are not generally exchanged during social occasions or in social situations. Instead, social business cards are exchanged. Social business cards are the same size as standard business cards (3 1/2" x 2"). They are usually white or ecru cards that are printed in black or grey ink. The cards are imprinted with your name and your office phone number. Your E-mail address may also be included.

"With Compliments" Cards:

"With Compliments" Cards (3 1/2" x 6 3/4") are used to forward an item of interest. They fold so that they may be attached to a magazine or annual report leaving exposed the words, "With compliments" or "For your interest" with your name imprinted below.

Memo Pads:

Memo pads (5" x 7") can be used to jot down notes during meetings and phone calls. Your name and, perhaps, your title appear at the top of each sheet.

Jotter Cards:

Jotter cards (3" x 5") fit inside leather carrying cases and travel with you to meetings and trade shows. They can also be kept readily available on your desk in an open-top holder. Jotter cards can double as business cards. Their extra space affords you the opportunity to jot down a reminder to your clients as to why they might want to get in touch with you on a specific matter.

Your name or name, address, and phone number appear at the top of each card.

Business Invitations:

Business invitations may be created for any type of corporate function from a grand opening or relocation of offices to a reception honoring a retiree or a top salesperson. They may be formal or informal, depending on the purpose of the event and the impression you want to create. Many times, a corporate logo is placed at the top of the invitation.

While it is impossible to include every type of invitation that you might use, almost any situation can be handled by looking at the samples provided and substituting your information for the information in the samples. For example, if your company, the XYZ Company, were hosting a dinner to honor the accomplishments of your senior editor, you might follow the format below, substituting your company's name on the invitation line, dinner for reception on Event Line 1, "in honor of" on Event Line 2, and your senior editor's name on Event Line 3.

By following this format, you can create copy for any type of invitation for any event. You can even start with this format and change the order in which the information is presented. The important thing is simply to make sure that all of the necessary information is included. See both sample #1 and sample #2 on next page.

Sample #1:

Invitation Line	Mr. Herbert Sanders
Request Line	requests the pleasure of your company
Event Line #1	at a reception
Event Line #2	to introduce the 2007 Holiday Line from
Event Line #3	Sharon Jay Togs
Date Line	Thursday, the fifth of April
Time Line	at seven o'clock
Location Line	The Red Lion Inn
Address Line	30 Main Street
City and State Line	Stockbridge, Massachusetts 01262
Reply Request Line	Please reply

Sample #2:

Event Line #2	To introduce the 2005 Holiday Line from
Event Line #3	Sharon Jay Togs
Invitation Line	Mr. Herbert Sanders
Request Line	requests the pleasure of your company
Event Line #1	at a reception
Date Line	Thursday, the third of April
Time Line	at seven o'clock
Location Line	New York Hilton
Address Line	Sixth Avenue at 53rd Street
City and State Line	New York, New York
Reply Request Line	Please reply

As you can see, all of the information is the same. It is just presented in a different sequence.

Business Announcements:

Business announcements are sent to inform clients of a change in the status of a company. Announcements may be sent for any number of reasons. The most popular reasons include a change of address, change of partners, introduction of a new officer, or even the introduction of a new product.

Business announcements are generally conservative unless the nature of your business allows for a flourish of creativity. As such, they are generally engraved in black ink on ecru or white card stock.

A rule of thumb: the name of a company is a singular entity that requires the use of a singular verb. For example:

Simpson, Healy Investments, Inc.
announces that its offices

or

Adamson and Shelton
is pleased to announce

Opening of an Office:

JOHN EVAN KAUFMAN, D.D.S.

ANNOUNCES THE OPENING OF HIS OFFICE

FOR THE

GENERAL PRACTICE OF DENTISTRY

PREVENTIVE · RESTORATIVE · COSMETIC

305 DEL MONTE BOULEVARD

SAN FRANCISCO, CALIFORNIA 94112

FOR APPOINTMENTS
(415) 555-1212

OFFICE HOURS
MONDAY - FRIDAY
8:00 TO 4:00

Relocation of Offices:

LAW OFFICES

HOUGHTON, WELMSLEY & HOWE

ANNOUNCES THAT THEIR OFFICES

ARE NOW LOCATED AT

56 OMEGA AVENUE

PROVIDENCE, RHODE ISLAND 02903

(410) 555-1212

Admittance of a New Associate:

Green&Hart

Green&Hart Investment Group

is pleased to announce that

Elizabeth Stokes Lindenman

has joined the company as

Vice President

65 Financial Place
New York, NY 10005

212 555-1212

Admittance of a New Partner:

Adamson and Shelton

Attorneys at Law

is pleased to announce that

David S. Clifford

has been admitted to the partnership

The firm name will now be known as

Adamson, Shelton and Clifford

1300 Walnut Street
Philadelphia, Pennsylvania 19107

(215) 555-1212

Formation of a Partnership:

Brian R. Toomey

and

Henry T. Warren

announce the formation of a partnership

for the general practice of law

under the firm name of

Toomey and Warren

725 Rio Grande Boulevard, N.W.
Albuquerque, New Mexico 87104   (505) 555-1212

Announcement of a Death:

It is with sadness that we

announce the death of

Jonathan Lewis Vorhees

Editor in Chief

November twenty-second

Two thousand and two

McCullough Publishing Company

WEDDING INVITATIONS AND ANNOUNCEMENTS

SELECTING YOUR WEDDING INVITATIONS

"First impressions count the most." You have probably heard that advice over and over again. It is sound advice and something to keep in mind when selecting wedding invitations. Since wedding invitations arrive weeks before the wedding, they set the tone for the wedding. In addition to informing your guests of the date, time and place, they subtly tell your guests how formal your wedding will be and how formally they should dress. They may even influence the types of gifts you receive.

Your invitations should be a reflection of your wedding. Traditional weddings and receptions call for traditional invitations. On the other hand, less formal invitations should be used for weddings held in less traditional settings.

Selecting wedding invitations requires asking five important questions:

1. What kind of paper should I use?
2. What color ink should I use?
3. Should my invitations be engraved or printed?
4. What lettering style should I use?
5. How should my invitations read?

The remainder of this chapter will attempt to answer those questions and help you select the stationery wardrobe that is most appropriate for you.

WHAT KIND OF PAPER SHOULD I USE?

This is actually a three-part question, as you need to choose the material from which the paper is made, the color, and whether to use a card or letter sheet.

Paper is made from either cotton or wood. The first true papers were made from cotton almost two thousand years ago. Wood-pulp papers came into being in the 1800s during the industrial revolution. They supplanted cotton-fiber papers for many uses because of their lower cost and the seemingly endless supply of trees.

The finest paper, though, is made from cotton. Before you order your stationery, run your fingers across the paper. Stationery made from cotton will have a soft, rich feel. You will undoubtedly recognize the quality inherent in cotton-fiber papers. Crane's 100% cotton fiber papers have the touch and feel of uncommonly beautiful papers.

Wedding invitations are printed on ecru (also known as buff, cream, and ivory) or white cards or letter sheets. The most traditional wedding invitations are printed on ecru or white letter sheets. Letter sheets have a fold on the left-hand side and open like a book. Only the front page is printed.

WHAT COLOR INK SHOULD I USE?

Formal wedding invitations are engraved in black. However, exceptionally bold lettering styles on white paper can look too heavy when engraved in black ink. In such cases, dark grey ink is suggested.

Less formal invitations today might incorporate other colors such as navy, burgundy or sage green. The color selection is often made to reflect the season or tone of the event, or to coordinate with the color palette of the wedding.

SHOULD MY INVITATIONS BE ENGRAVED OR PRINTED?

Wedding invitations and announcements can be engraved, thermographed, or flat-printed.

Engraving is one of the oldest and most beautiful processes for reproducing images on paper. The appeal of engraving lies in the exquisite detail created by its three-dimensional impression. Engraving is produced when the copy is etched in reverse into a copper plate. Ink is deposited in the resulting cavity. The engraving press then forces the paper into the cavity, creating a raised impression. The paper is literally raised with the ink adhering to the raised surface. The fact that the paper is raised is what distinguishes engraving from thermography and flat-printing.

It is easy to tell whether or not wedding invitations are engraved. Simply turn one over. If there is an indentation (caused by the pressure from the engraving press), it is engraved. You can also tell by looking closely at the impression on the front. The paper will be smoother there and there may be a little ripple to the sheet. This is called the "bruise" and is a natural part of the process.

Thermography is sometimes called "raised printing," although the printing is not raised at all. Unlike engraving, where the paper is actually raised, the raise in thermography is created by a resinous powder that is melted over the flat-printed ink. Thermography is less expensive than engraving but, while quite handsome, is not quite as appealing.

Flat-printed, as its name implies, is simply ink applied to a flat surface with no raise.

CHOOSING A LETTERING STYLE

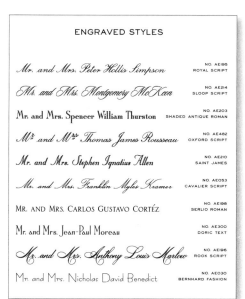

ENGRAVED STYLES

Mr. and Mrs. Peter Hollis Simpson — NO. AE195 ROYAL SCRIPT

Mr. and Mrs. Montgomery McKeon — NO. AE214 SLOOP SCRIPT

Mr. and Mrs. Spencer William Thurston — NO. AE203 SHADED ANTIQUE ROMAN

Mr. and Mrs. Thomas James Rousseau — NO. AE482 OXFORD SCRIPT

Mr. and Mrs. Stephen Ignatius Allen — NO. AE210 SAINT JAMES

Mr. and Mrs. Franklin Myles Kramer — NO. AE053 CAVALIER SCRIPT

MR. AND MRS. CARLOS GUSTAVO CORTÉZ — NO. AE198 SERLIO ROMAN

Mr. and Mrs. Jean-Paul Moreau — NO. AE300 DORIC TEXT

Mr. and Mrs. Anthony Louis Marlow — NO. AE196 ROOK SCRIPT

Mr. and Mrs. Nicholas David Benedict — NO. AE030 BERNHARD FASHION

There are literally hundreds of different lettering styles to choose from. Fortunately, most stationers limit your choices.

You should choose a lettering style that fits both the formality of the wedding and your personal taste. Your stationer can show you different styles, suggest the appropriate ones, and tell you which ones are most popular. Ultimately, you will decide according to your personal taste.

HOW SHOULD MY INVITATIONS READ?

The composition of traditional wedding invitations was once governed by strict rules of etiquette. Changing family structures and a general trend toward more informality has created a need to relax some of the rules of etiquette. This chapter discusses both the traditional wording of wedding invitations and some suggested alternatives.

Traditional Wording:

Invitational Line	Mr. and Mrs. Paul James Tavis
Request Line	request the honour of your presence
Event Line	at the marriage of their daughter
Bride's Name	Christina Lee
Joining Word	and
Groom's Name	Mr. Andrew Jay Finnin
Date Line	Saturday, the second of June
Year Line	Two thousand and seven
Time Line	at six o'clock
Location	Old First Presbyterian Church
Address	125 Main Street
City and State	Huntington, New York

INVITATIONAL LINE

The invitational line tells your guests who is extending the invitation. Traditionally, wedding invitations were sent only by the bride's parents. While the parents of the bride still issue the invitations to most weddings, many are now issued by combinations of the bride's parents and step-parents along with the groom's parents and step-parents. Sometimes, even the bride and groom themselves are added to the mix. This is being done for a number of reasons, among them is the need to accommodate divorces and remarriages.

Regardless of who is issuing the invitations, convention dictates the way in which proper names appear. One very important rule to remember is that no abbreviations are used on traditional wedding invitations. Titles such as "Mr." and "Mrs." are properly abbreviated but names are not. Men and women use their full social names, including middle names. If a gentleman insists on not using his middle name, it is better to omit it entirely than to use his initial.

Bride's Married Parents:

When the bride's parents are married to each other, their names appear together on the first line of the invitations. They use their titles, followed by the husband's full name.

Mr. and Mrs. Paul James Travis

Bride's Father is a Medical Doctor:

The use of "Doctor" on formal invitations is generally reserved for medical doctors and ministers with advanced degrees. (PhD's properly use their titles only in academic settings.) When the bride's father is a medical doctor, he uses his professional title. "Doctor" is properly written out, but he may abbreviate it if he has an unusually long name.

Doctor and Mrs. Paul James Travis

Dr. and Mrs. Paul James Travis

Bride's Mother is a Medical Doctor:

Traditionally, the bride's mother uses her social title - "Mrs." - so the invitational line should read "Mr. and Mrs. Paul James Travis". However, many women now prefer to use their professional titles so the etiquette is changing. The best way to display the mother's title is to show it on the first line of the invitation with her husband's name on the second line, preceded by the word "and". The use of "and" indicates that they are married. (The names are shown on separate lines because they would not comfortably fit together on a single line.) There are other possible presentations but all of them are awkward. For example, you may see "Mr. and Dr. Paul James Travis" used. This seems like a possible solution until you remove the "Mr. and" and are left with "Dr. Paul James Travis", who is obviously not the mother.

Dr. Laura Simpson Travis
and Mr. Paul James Travis

Both Parents are Medical Doctors:

When both parents are medical doctors, their names properly read "Doctor and Mrs." Acceptable alternatives include "The Doctors Travis" and displaying the parents' names on separate lines.

Doctor Laura Simpson Travis
and Doctor Paul James Travis

Bride's Father is a Minister:

Ordained ministers may use their clerical titles. He generally uses "The Reverend" unless he holds a doctorate in which case he is "The Reverend Doctor". The titles are never abbreviated. If the invitational line becomes too long, his title may appear alone on the first line.

The Reverend and Mrs. Paul James Travis

The Reverend Doctor
and Mrs. Paul James Travis

Bride's Mother is a Minister:

Traditionally, the bride's mother uses her social title - "Mrs." - so the invitational line should read "Mr. and Mrs. Paul James Travis". However, many women now prefer to use their professional titles so the etiquette is changing. The best way to display the mother's title is to show it on the first line of the invitation with her husband's name on the second line, preceded by the word "and". The use of "and" indicates that they are married. (The names are shown on separate lines because they would not comfortably fit together on a single line.)

The Reverend Laura Simpson Travis
and Mr. Paul James Travis

Both Parents are Ministers:

When both parents are ordained ministers, their names properly read, "The Reverend and Mrs." Acceptable alternatives include "The Reverends Travis" and placing their names on separate lines.

The Reverend Laura Simpson Travis

and The Reverend Paul James Travis

Bride's Father is a Judge:

When the bride's father is a judge, he generally refers to himself as "Judge". He may, instead, use "The Honorable" although that is a title that is bestowed upon him by others and may be considered presumptuous when applied to oneself.

Judge and Mrs. Paul James Travis

The Honorable Paul James Travis and Mrs. Travis

Bride's Mother is a Judge:

Traditionally, the bride's mother uses her social title - "Mrs." - so the invitational line should read "Mr. and Mrs. Paul James Travis". However, many women now prefer to use their titles so the etiquette is changing. The best way to display the mother's title is to show it on the first line of the invitation with her husband's name on the second line, preceded by the word "and". The use of "and" indicates that they are married. (The names are shown on separate lines because they would not comfortably fit together on a single line.) The bride's mother would refer to herself as "Judge". She may, instead, use "The Honorable" although that is a title that is bestowed upon her by others and may be considered presumptuous when applied to oneself.

Judge Laura Simpson Travis
and Mr. Paul James Travis

The Honorable Laura Simpson Travis
and Mr. Paul James Travis

Both Parents are Judges:

When both parents are judges, their names properly read, "Judge and Mrs." Acceptable alternatives include "The Judges Travis" and using "The Honorable" in front of both names (although that might seem presumptuous). When this is done, their names appear on separate lines.

The Judges Travis

Judge Laura Simpson Travis
and Judge Paul James Travis

The Honorable Laura Simpson Travis
and The Honorable Paul James Travis

Bride's and Groom's Families Share Costs:

Traditionally, the invitation is issued in the bride's parents' names. Today, if the bride would like to include the groom's parents' names in issuing the invitation, their names may be used on the invitational lines. The bride's parents' names appear on the first line. The names of the groom's parents appear on the second line. In situations where the parents are divorced, there may be too many names to list at the top of the invitation. In such a case, the bride and groom may issue the invitations along with their parents as in the samples below.

Miss Christina Lee Travis
and
Mr. Andrew Jay Fannin
together with their parents

or

Miss Christina Lee Travis
and
Mr. Andrew Jay Fannin
together with their families

Divorced Parents:

Many emotions are involved when dealing with divorced parents and their spouses. When handled with love and understanding, few problems arise. While there are prescribed rules of etiquette for such situations, adherence to these rules may hurt the feelings of somebody you love. It is always better to "break" a rule when the alternative is to make a family member feel unimportant or unwanted. While this section will discuss the traditional way to present the names of divorced parents, remember that it may be desirable for you to alter that presentation.

Since wedding invitations are properly issued only by the bride's natural parents (unless she has been legally adopted), only the names of the bride's natural parents properly appear on the invitations. In other words, step-parents names are not used. (There are a couple of exceptions which will be discussed in the next section.)

The name of the bride's mother appears on the first line. Her father's name appears on line two. The lines are not separated by "and" since that would indicate that they are married.

Divorced women use their first name, maiden name, and surname, preceded by "Mrs." If she has remarried, she uses her husband's full name. preceded by "Mrs."

If the bride's mother has resumed the use of her maiden name, she uses her first name, middle name, and maiden name. No titles are used on the invitation.

Bride's Mother has not Remarried:

Mrs. Laura Simpson Travis
Mr. Paul James Travis

Bride's Mother has Remarried:

Mrs. Glenn Lincoln Sanderson
Mr. Paul James Travis

Bride's Mother has Resumed Use of Maiden Name:

Laura Lynn Simpson
Paul James Travis

Step-Parents:

The rule governing the use of step-parents' names states that only the names of the bride's natural parents (unless she has been legally adopted) properly appear on traditional wedding invitations. Exceptions occur when the bride's step-parent helped raise her from a young age, and when the bride feels especially close to her step-parent.

The invitational line reads "Mr. and Mrs." followed by the husband's full name. The event line mentions whose daughter is being married. The bride uses her full name, without a title, when her mother and step-father issue the invitations. When the invitations are issued by her father and step-mother, she uses just her first and middle names.

Bride's Mother and Step-Father:

> *Mr. and Mrs. Glenn Lincoln Sanderson*
> *request the honour of your presence*
> *at the marriage of Mrs. Sanderson's daughter*
> *Christina Lee Travis*

or, less formally

> *Mr. and Mrs. Glenn Lincoln Sanderson*
> *request the honour of your presence*
> *at the marriage of her daughter*
> *Christina Lee Travis*

Bride's Father and Step-Mother:

> *Mr. and Mrs. Paul James Travis*
> *request the honour of your presence*
> *at the marriage of Mr. Travis's daughter*
> *Christina Lee*

or, less formally

> *Mr. and Mrs. Paul James Travis*
> *request the honour of your presence*
> *at the marriage of his daughter*
> *Christina Lee*

Separated Parents:

Parents who are legally separated have two options: They may follow the format for married parents or, if they prefer, the format for divorced parents. The bride's mother uses either "Mrs." followed by her husband's full name or her first name, maiden name, and married name, without her title. If the bride's mother does not use her title, the bride's father and the groom omit their titles as well.

Widowed Parents:

When one of the bride's parents is deceased, the name of the surviving parent appears alone on the invitational line. Widows continue to use their husband's full name, preceded by "Mrs." If she remarries, she uses "Mrs." followed by her present husband's name. In this case, the bride uses her full name without her title. The name of the deceased spouse is not mentioned on the invitation. His or her name does appear in the newspaper announcement and may appear in the wedding program or, perhaps, in a prayer said during the ceremony.

Widows may use "senior" after their names when they have a son who is a "junior." This will avoid confusing her with her daughter-in-law. When "senior" is spelled out, a lower case "s" is used. When abbreviated, the "S" is capitalized.

Widowers use their full name, preceded by their title.

Bride's Mother has not Remarried:

Mrs. Paul James Travis

Bride's Mother has Remarried:

Mrs. Glenn Lincoln Sanderson
requests the pleasure of your company
at the marriage of her daughter
Christina Lee Travis

Bride's Father:

Mr. Paul James Travis

Persons Other Than the Bride's Parents:

Another member of the bride's family or any close friend may host the wedding. This might occur when the bride's parents are no longer alive. When relatives issue the invitations, their relationship to the bride is mentioned on the event line. The bride's full name appears on the following line, without her title. When friends issue the invitations, the event line reads, "at the marriage of". The bride uses her full name including her title.

Bride's Relative:

Mrs. Jeffrey Harold Travis
requests the honour of your presence
at the marriage of her granddaughter
Christina Lee Travis

Mr. and Mrs. John Kevin Murphey
request the honour of your presence
at the marriage of
Miss Christina Lee Travis

Parents of the Groom:

When the bride's parents are deceased or when they live out of the country, the groom's parents might host the wedding. When this is done, the parents' relationship to the groom is mentioned on the fifth line instead of on the third. This wording preserves the tradition of the bride being married to the groom. Both the bride and the groom use their full names, preceded by their titles.

Mr. and Mrs. John Carlton Fannin
request the honour of your presence
at the marriage of
Miss Christina Lee Travis
to their son
Mr. Andrew Jay Fannin

Bride and Groom:

The bride and groom may issue the invitations to their wedding. This might be the case for a marriage of an older couple or a second marriage. (However, regardless of the circumstances, it is always nice to have the bride's parents issue the invitations. This shows that the parents approve of the marriage - and that they are alive.) There are two formats that might be used. The more formal one dispenses with the invitational line while the less formal, more popular one, follows the traditional sequence.

Most Formal:

The honour of your presence
is requested at the marriage of
Miss Christina Lee Travis
to
Mr. Andrew Jay Fannin

Less Formal:

Miss Christina Lee Travis
and
Mr. Andrew Jay Fannin
request the honour of your presence
at their marriage

Second Marriages:

When a woman is marrying for the second time, the couple generally issues their own invitations. The bride uses her present name. A divorced woman uses her first name, maiden name, and married name or her maiden name, if she has resumed using it. Neither the bride nor the groom use titles. A widow uses her present married name, including her title. The bride's parents may issue the invitations for a young bride who is widowed. In this case, the bride uses her full married name, without titles.

A woman marrying for a third time uses her first name, maiden name, and current last name.

Divorced Bride:

The honour of your presence
is requested at the marriage of
Christina Travis Mackay
to
Andrew Jay Fannin

or, less formally

Christina Travis Mackay
and
Andrew Jay Fannin
request the honour of your presence
at their marriage

Widowed Bride:

The honour of your presence
is requested at the marriage of
Mrs. Laurence Nelson Mackay
to
Mr. Andrew Jay Fannin

or, less formally

Mrs. Laurence Nelson Mackay
and
Mr. Andrew Jay Fannin
request the honour of your presence
at their marriage

Young Widow:

Mr. and Mrs. Paul James Travis
request the honour of your presence
at the marriage of their daughter
Christina Travis Mackay

REQUEST LINE

The request line invites your guests to your wedding. The wording varies according to where your wedding is being held and what type of service it is. "Request the honour (or honor) of your presence" is always used when the wedding ceremony is being held in a house of worship as you cannot request the pleasure of one's company in God's house. Weddings held at a club, reception hall, or home generally use "request the pleasure of your company." However, if it is a religious ceremony "request the honour of your presence" may be used. When using the English spelling of "honour", the spelling of "favour", if used, should follow suit.

"Request the pleasure of your company" is always used for civil ceremonies.

Religious Ceremony:

request the honour of your presence

Civil Ceremony:

request the pleasure of your company

The bride uses only her first name and middle name on invitations issued by her parents. She uses neither her title nor her surname since it is assumed that she has never married and has the same last name as her parents. The bride uses her full name when her last name is different from the last name of whoever issues the invitations. When a woman is marrying for the second time, she uses her present name. A divorced woman uses her first name, maiden name, and married name or her maiden name, if she has resumed using it. She does not use her title. A woman who had a previous marriage annulled, may use "Miss." A widow uses her present married name, including her title. However, a young widow may use her first name, maiden name, and surname, without her title.

When Issued by the Bride's Parents:
Christina Lee

When the Bride is a Medical Doctor:
Doctor Christina Lee Travis

When Issued by the Bride's Mother and Stepfather:
Christina Lee Travis

When Issued by a First-Time Bride and Groom:
Miss Christina Lee Travis

When Issued by a Previously Divorced Bride and Groom:
Christina Travis Mackay

When Issued by a Widowed Bride and Groom:
Mrs. Laurence Nelson Mackay

When Issued by the Parents of a Young Widow:
Christina Travis Mackay

When Issued by the Parents of a Woman Whose First Marriage was Annulled:
Christina Lee Travis

JOINING WORD

The word "to" is used to join the names of the bride and groom on invitations to the wedding ceremony. "And" is used to join the name of the bride and groom on invitations to a nuptial mass and on invitations to a wedding reception.

GROOM'S NAME

The groom always uses his full name, preceded by his title. Names and titles, except "Mr." are always spelled out, never abbreviated or replaced with an initial. If the groom feels that his middle name is distasteful and refuses to use it, he should omit it entirely.

Use of "Junior":

A man is a junior when he shares the same name as his father. He uses junior until his father passes away. At that point, he drops it from his name. If, however, his father were a well-known figure, he would continue to use "junior" to avoid any confusion. Although it is acceptable to abbreviate "junior", its proper usage is to spell it out. When spelled out, it is used with a lower case "j". When abbreviated, an upper case "J" is used. A comma always precedes "junior" whether written out or abbreviated.

Mr. Andrew Jay Fannin, junior

Mr. Andrew Jay Fannin, Jr.

Use of "II" and "III":

"II" is used by a man who shares the same name as an older relative who is not his father while "III" is used by a man who is named after somebody who uses "junior" or "II". When used on invitations, a comma usually precedes the "II" or "III" although it is equally acceptable to omit it.

Mr. Andrew Jay Fannin, III

Mr. Andrew Jay Fannin III

Use of "Esquire":

"Esquire" is a title that is used by some lawyers to indicate their profession. Meaning "gentleman", its origin is England where it is used as a term of deference when referring to somebody else. It is not recognized as a proper social title in the United States and, therefore, is not properly used on formal wedding invitations.

DATE LINE

The day of the week and the date of the month are given on this line. Each word and numeral is spelled out. The day of the week may be preceded by "on" but it is more frequently left off. The time of day, as in "Saturday evening" may be included. That is usually not necessary as most guests will be able to determine the time of day without that additional information. Times that might require clarification are nine o'clock and ten o'clock.

Saturday, the sixth of June

on Saturday, the sixth of June

Saturday evening, the sixth of June

YEAR LINE

Due to the immediacy of the event, it is not necessary to include the year on your wedding invitations. Since your invitations are mailed four to six weeks before the wedding, your guests will know that your wedding will take place on the following June sixth. However, it is not improper to include the year and it might be a thoughtful thing to do since many guests will save your invitations. One word of caution: Many lettering styles, especially scripts, look better with fewer lines of copy. You might want to ask to see a proof before adding the year to your invitations.

The first word in the year line is capitalized.

Two thousand and seven

TIME LINE

The time always appears on one line, preceded by "at". No upper case letters are used. Twelve o'clock noon is expressed simply as "twelve o'clock". Your guests will assume that your wedding is taking place at noon and not at midnight.

The time line can also be used to indicate the time of the day. "In the morning", "in the afternoon", and "in the evening" may follow the time. They are not used, however, when the time of day is shown on the date line.

at six o'clock

at half after six o'clock

at three quarters after six o'clock

at six o'clock in the evening

LOCATION

The name of the facility at which your wedding will take place is shown on the location line. The complete name of the facility is given. If the word "Saint" is part of the church's name, it should be spelled out. Sometimes a church commonly known as "Saint Michael's Church" might actually be named "Church of Saint Michael". You may also want to include the denomination of the church. This is helpful when there are both Catholic and Episcopal churches of the same name. It is best to check with a member of the clergy or with the church secretary to ascertain the correct name of the church.

STREET ADDRESS

The street address is necessary only when there is more than one facility with the same name in the same town. It is also included when the facility is not well-known and there are a large number of out-of-town guests. The street address is not included when maps or direction cards are included.

CITY AND STATE

The names of the city and state in which the wedding is being held are shown on the last line of the invitation. The city comes first, followed by the state. They are separated by a comma. Exceptions to this rule include weddings being held in New York City and in Washington, D.C. Since "New York, New York" may seem redundant, it is correct to use either "New York City" or just "New York". Weddings held in the District of Columbia use either "City of Washington" or "Washington, District of Columbia".

CEREMONY AND RECEPTION HELD AT THE SAME LOCATION

When both the wedding ceremony and reception are held at the same location, the last line of the invitation reads either "and afterwards at the reception" or "and afterward at the reception".

Mr. and Mrs. Paul James Travis
request the honour of your presence
at the marriage of their daughter
Christina Lee
to
Mr. Andrew Jay Fannin
Saturday, the sixth of June
at six o'clock
Old First Presbyterian Church
Huntington, New York
and afterwards at the reception

HISPANIC WEDDINGS

Invitations to an Hispanic wedding are issued by both sets of parents. There are several traditional formats. One format calls for the bride's parents to issue their invitation on the left-inside page while the groom's parents issue theirs on the right-inside page. Common information, such as the date, time, and place are combined in the center of the invitation across the fold.

The invitations may also be issued jointly by both sets of parents on a single page. In this format, the names of the bride's father and mother appear on the first two lines. "And" appears on the third line with the names of the groom's father and mother on lines four and five.

The invitations may also be engraved in two languages; Spanish on the left-inside and English on the right-inside.

Customs do vary from one nationality to another. Any questions concerning appropriate etiquette in a given country are best answered by calling the protocol officer in the respective consulate.

José Hernandez Caratini
Carmen Maria de Hernandez
request the honour of your presence
at the marriage of their daughter
Linda
to
Roberto Martinez

Juan Martinez Garza
Consuela Elena de Martinez
request the honour of your presence
at the marriage of
Linda Hernandez
to their son
Roberto

Saturday, the twelfth of July
Two thousand and three
at two o'clock
Santa Iglesia Cathedral
San Juan, Puerto Rico

NUPTIAL MASS

A Nuptial Mass is a Catholic Mass celebrating a wedding. Nuptial Masses are about an hour long. Your invitations should mention that a Nuptial Mass is being performed as that will notify your guests that the ceremony might be a little longer than others they have attended. Since the wording indicates that the bride and groom are being joined together, "and" is used, instead of "to".

Mr. and Mrs. Paul James Travis
request the honour of your presence
at the Nuptial Mass uniting their daughter
Christina Lee
and
Mr. Andrew Jay Fannin
in the Sacrament of Holy Matrimony
Saturday, the sixth of June
at ten o'clock
Saint Patrick's Cathedral
New York

JEWISH WEDDINGS

In contrast to Christian tradition, where the bride's family gives the bride away, the Jewish tradition celebrates the uniting of the two families. Therefore, the names of both sets of parents correctly appear on the invitations. The names of the bride's parents appear at the top of the invitations. The names of the groom's parents appear either at the top beneath the bride's parents' names or after the groom's name on two lines reading, "son of / Dr. and Mrs. Richard Samuel Abrams". The bride's surname is used when the names of both sets of parents appear at the top of the invitations.

Mr. and Mrs. Howard Blumberg
Dr. and Mrs. David Green
request the honour of your presence
at the marriage of
Sarah Blumberg
to
William Greenspan
Sunday, the tenth of May
at eight o'clock
Temple Sholom
Chicago, Illinois

Mr. and Mrs. Howard Blumberg
request the honour of your presence
at the marriage of their daughter
Sarah
to
Mr. William Greenspan
son of
Dr. and Mrs. David Greenspan
Sunday, the tenth of May
at eight o'clock
Temple Sholom
Chicago, Illinois

MORMON WEDDINGS

Members of the Church of Jesus Christ of Latter-day Saints are married or "sealed for time and all eternity" in temples open only to practicing Latter-day Saints. The ceremonies are small with larger receptions afterward. Since more guests are invited to the reception than to the ceremony, invitations are issued to the reception with ceremony cards enclosed with the invitations sent to those invited to the ceremony. Because of the importance of eternal families in the Mormon religion, the groom's parents are honored by having their names included on the invitations. Their names appear beneath the groom's name.

Reception Invitation:

Mr. and Mrs. Paul James Travis
request the pleasure of your company
at the marriage reception of their daughter
Christina Lee
and
Mr. Andrew Jay Fannin
following their marriage
in the Bountiful L.D.S. Temple
Saturday, the sixth of June
at seven o'clock
La Caille at Quail Run
Salt Lake City, Utah

Ceremony Card:

The honour of your presence is requested
at the Temple Ceremony
Saturday, the sixth of June
at six o'clock
Bountiful L.D.S. Temple

DOUBLE WEDDING CEREMONY

The elder sister's name appears first on invitations for a double wedding ceremony for two sisters. When a double wedding is performed for brides who are not related, separate invitations are sent.

Mr. and Mrs. Paul James Travis
request the honour of your presence
at the marriage of their daughters
Christina Lee

to

Mr. Andrew Jay Fannin

and

Alexandra Noel

to

Mr. Robert Stuart Martin
Saturday, the sixth of June
at six o'clock
Old First Presbyterian Church
Huntington, New York

PERSONALIZED WEDDING INVITATIONS

As with any invitation, the most formal wording allows space to write in the name of the guest. This format gives special honor to your guests. Their names are calligraphed on the invitations. Personalized invitations can also be used in lieu of an admission card.

Mr. and Mrs. Paul James Travis
request the honour of the presence of
Mr. and Mrs. Nicholas Jude Flanagan
at the marriage of their daughter
Christina Lee

INVITATION TO A WEDDING HELD AT HOME

When a wedding is being held at the home of the person(s) extending the invitation (your parents' home, for example), their address appears on the location line. "Request the pleasure of your company" is generally used although you may use "request the honour of your presence" if you are having a religious ceremony.

Mr. and Mrs. Paul James Travis
request the pleasure of your company
at the marriage of their daughter
Christina Lee
to
Mr. Andrew Jay Fannin
Saturday, the sixth of June
at six o'clock
307 West Shore Road
Huntington, New York

INVITATION TO A WEDDING HELD AT THE RESIDENCE OF...

A wedding held at the home of someone other than the person(s) who are issuing the invitations requires a line reading "at the residence of" followed by a line with the names of the people at whose home the wedding is being held. Their address is given on the next two lines. "Request the pleasure of your company" is generally used although you may use "request the honour of your presence" if you are having a religious ceremony.

Mr. and Mrs. Paul James Travis
request the pleasure of your company
at the marriage of their daughter
Christina Lee
to
Mr. Andrew Jay Fannin
Saturday, the sixth of June
at six o'clock
at the residence of
Mr. and Mrs. Robert Anthony Dignon
106 Cove Road
Huntington, New York

INVITATIONS TO A MARRIAGE RECEPTION

Invitations to a marriage reception are sent when more people are invited to the reception than to the ceremony. Ceremony cards are enclosed with the invitations sent to those guests who are also invited to the wedding ceremony.

Ceremony cards are the size of standard reception cards and are formally worded as though they are separate invitations (which they are). The names of the location, city, and state are omitted when they would repeat information from the reception invitations.

The word "wedding" may be substituted for "marriage". The word "and" replaces "to" on reception invitations.

Reception Invitation:

Mr. and Mrs. Paul James Travis
request the pleasure of your company
at the marriage reception of their daughter
Christina Lee
and
Mr. Andrew Jay Fannin
Saturday, the sixth of June
at seven o'clock
Cold Spring Harbor Country Club
Cold Spring Harbor, New York

Ceremony Card:

Mr. and Mrs. Paul James Travis
request the honour of your presence
at the marriage ceremony
Saturday, the sixth of June
at six o'clock
Old First Presbyterian Church

or

The honour of your presence
is requested at the marriage ceremony
Saturday, the sixth of June
at six o'clock
Old First Presbyterian Church

INVITATIONS TO A LATE RECEPTION

Receptions held after the day of the wedding are not properly considered wedding receptions. Instead, they are referred to as parties in honor of the married couple. They may be given for any reason, but are usually given when the wedding is held in a town other than the one in which the bride's and groom's family and friends live. They are also frequently held after a second marriage. Since late receptions are separate events, they require their own invitation and mailing.

Mr. and Mrs. John Carlton Fannin
request the pleasure of your company
at a dinner party in honor of
Mr. and Mrs. Andrew Jay Fannin
Saturday, the twenty-second of August
at eight o'clock
3608 Clubhouse Lane
Boca Raton, Florida

HANDWRITTEN INVITATIONS

The most personal wedding invitations are handwritten. If you are having a small wedding, you might want to hand-write your invitations. Handwritten invitations may follow the standard wedding invitation format or they can be personal letters sent to each of your guests telling them that you are getting married and what the specifics are. The formality of the wording varies according to your closeness to the guests.

Handwritten invitations are written in black or dark blue ink on ecru or white letter sheets. Letter sheets are formal sheets of paper with a fold along the left-hand side (like standard wedding invitations). They fold in half again from top to bottom and are mailed in envelopes that are slightly larger than half the size of the sheet. Traditionally, the stationery is unadorned at the top. In other words, it is plain with no name, monogram, or coat of arms.

Dear Aunt Regina and Uncle Allen,

Paul and I will be getting married on Saturday, the sixth of June at six o'clock at Old First Presbyterian Church. The reception will be held afterwards at the Club.

We want you to be a part of our special day.

Love,
Christina

MILITARY WEDDINGS

Invitations for weddings involving members of the United States armed forces follow the same etiquette as civilian weddings, with the exception of the use of military titles and service designations. Unless necessary because of space limitations, military titles are never abbreviated.

Army, Air Force, and Marine officers with the rank of Captain and higher use their military titles before their names. Their service designation appears on a separate line beneath their name and rank. An exception is when invitations are issued by an officer and his wife, in which case the service designation line is omitted.

Navy and Coast Guard officers with the rank of Commander and higher use their military titles before their names. Their service designation appears on a separate line beneath their name and rank. An exception is when invitations are issued by an officer and his wife, in which case the service designation line is omitted.

Junior officers do not use their titles (neither military nor civilian) before their names. Their titles appear on the following line, before their service designation.

Non-commissioned officers show only their service designations. Their rank does not appear on invitations.

High ranking officers who retire continue to use their military titles. Their retired status is noted after their service designation. When their service designation is not used, as on invitations issued by a retired Colonel and his wife, the officer's retired status is not mentioned.

The guide below indicates how specific situations are properly handled.

PARENTS OF THE BRIDE

Parents are Married:

Father is an Officer:
> Colonel and Mrs. Paul James Travis

Father is a Junior Officer:
> Lieutenant and Mrs. Paul James Travis

Father is a Non-Commissioned Officer or Enlisted Man:
> Mr. and Mrs. Paul James Travis

Father is a Retired Officer:
> Colonel and Mrs. Paul James Travis

Mother is an Officer:
> Mr. and Mrs. Paul James Travis

or

> Colonel Laura Simpson Travis
> United States Army
> and Mr. Paul James Travis

Mother is a Junior Officer:
> Mr. and Mrs. Paul James Travis

or

> Laura Simpson Travis
> Lieutenant, United States Army
> and Mr. Paul James Travis

Mother is a Non-Commissioned Officer or Enlisted Woman:
> Mr. and Mrs. Paul James Travis

or

> Laura Simpson Travis
> United States Army
> and Mr. Paul James Travis

Mother is a Retired Officer:
> Mr. and Mrs. Paul James Travis

or

> Colonel Laura Simpson Travis
> United States Army, Retired
> and Mr. Paul James Travis

Both Parents are Officers:

Colonel and Mrs. Paul James Travis

or

The Colonels Travis

or

Colonel Laura Simpson Travis
United States Army
and Colonel Paul James Travis
United States Army

Parents are Divorced:

Father is an Officer:

Mrs. Laura Simpson Travis
Colonel Paul James Travis
United States Army

Father is a Junior Officer:

Mrs. Laura Simpson Travis
Paul James Travis
Lieutenant, United States Army

Father is a Non-Commissioned Officer or Enlisted Man:

Mrs. Laura Simpson Travis
Paul James Travis
United States Army

Father is a Retired Officer:

Mrs. Laura Simpson Travis
Colonel Paul James Travis
United States Army, Retired

Mother is an Officer:

Colonel Laura Simpson Travis
United States Army
Mr. Paul James Travis

Mother is a Junior Officer:

Laura Simpson Travis
Lieutenant, United States Army
Mr. Paul James Travis

Mother is a Non-Commissioned Officer or Enlisted Woman:

Laura Simpson Travis
United States Army
Mr. Paul James Travis

Mother is a Retired Officer:

Colonel Laura Simpson Travis
United States Army, Retired
Mr. Paul James Travis

Both Parents are Officers:

Colonel Laura Simpson Travis
United States Army
Colonel Paul James Travis
United States Army

BRIDE'S NAME

Officer:

Commander Christina Lee Travis
United States Navy

Junior Officer:

Christina Lee Travis
Ensign, United States Navy

Non-Commissioned Officer or Enlisted Woman:

Christina Lee Travis
United States Navy

GROOM'S NAME

Officer:

Major Andrew Jay Fannin
United States Marine Corps

Junior Officer:

Andrew Jay Fannin
First Lieutenant, United States Marine Corps

Non-Commissioned Officer or Enlisted Man:

Andrew Jay Fannin
United States Marine Corps

POSTPONEMENT OF A WEDDING

A wedding may need to be postponed due to illness or an unexpected death in the family. When there is enough time to do so, formal announcements may be sent. If you do not have enough time to send formal announcements, you may notify your guests by phone.

Mr. and Mrs. Paul James Travis
announce that the marriage of their daughter
Christina Lee

to

Mr. Andrew James Fannin
has been postponed to
Saturday, the sixteenth of August
at six o'clock
Old First Presbyterian Church
Huntington, New York

INVITATION RECALLED

Wedding invitations are recalled when a wedding is postponed before a new date is set. New invitations are sent once new arrangements have been made. If there is not enough time to send a formal recall announcement, phone calls will suffice.

Recall Announcement:

Mr. and Mrs. Paul James Travis
regret that the illness of their daughter
Christina Lee
obliges them to recall their invitations
to her marriage to
Mr. Andrew Jay Fannin
on Saturday, the sixth of June

New Invitation:

Mr. and Mrs. Paul James Travis
announce that the wedding of their daughter
Christina Lee

to

Mr. Andrew Jay Fannin
which was postponed, will now take place
on Saturday, the sixteenth of August
at six o'clock
Old First Presbyterian Church
Huntington, New York

CANCELLATION OF A WEDDING

When a wedding needs to be canceled, formal announcements may be sent. If there is not enough time to send announcements, phone calls may be made instead.

Mr. and Mrs. Paul James Travis
are obliged to recall their invitations
to the marriage of their daughter
Christina Lee
to Mr. Andrew Jay Fannin
as the marriage will not take place

WEDDING ANNOUNCEMENTS

Wedding announcements are sent to family members, friends, and business associates who were not invited to your wedding. They are traditionally sent by the bride's parents but, many times, are sent by the bride and groom themselves. Announcements are always sent after the wedding, never before. They are usually sent the day after the wedding but may be sent up to one year afterward. They do not obligate the recipients to send gifts.

Traditional announcements, like the invitations, are engraved in black ink on ecru or white letter sheets and are mailed in double envelopes.

Wedding announcements follow the same etiquette as wedding invitations, although the wording is, of course, different. The parents of the bride always "have the honour" of announcing the marriage. The bride and groom simply "announce" their marriage. Parents should never omit "have the honour" as that might imply their disapproval.

Weddings held at a house of worship include its name. When weddings are held in locations other than houses of worship, the location is left off.

Since wedding announcements are sent after the wedding has taken place, it is necessary to include the year.

Invitations to social events, such as a late reception, are not properly included with wedding announcements. If you are planning a late reception, send separate invitations.

Issued by Parents:

Mr. and Mrs. Paul James Travis
have the honour of announcing
the marriage of their daughter
Christina Lee
to
Mr. Andrew Jay Fannin
Saturday, the sixth of June
Two thousand and seven
Old First Presbyterian Church
Huntington, New York

Issued by Bride and Groom:

Miss Christina Lee Travis
and
Mr. Andrew Jay Fannin
announce their marriage
Saturday, the sixth of June
Two thousand and seven
Old First Presbyterian Church
Huntington, New York

or, less formally

Christina Lee Travis
and
Andrew Jay Fannin
announce their marriage
Saturday, the sixth of June
Two thousand and seven
Old First Presbyterian Church
Huntington, New York

RECEPTION CARDS

Reception cards are sent with wedding invitations whenever the ceremony and reception are held in different places. They invite your guests to the reception and give them pertinent information, such as the time and place. (They already know the date.) Like the invitations, there is a standard format.

Occasion Line	*Reception*
Time Line	*immediately following the ceremony*
Location Line	*Cold Spring Harbor Country Club*
City and State Line	*Cold Spring Harbor, New York*
Reply Request	*R.s.v.p.*
	307 West Shore Road
	Huntington, New York 11743

Occasion Line:

The occasion line tells your guests what event it is that they are invited to. Receptions take place at one o'clock in the afternoon or later. Breakfasts (regardless of the menu) are held before one o'clock, although "Breakfast" is rarely used anymore on reception cards. If dinner is being served, you might want to use "Dinner Reception" or even "Dinner and Dancing" to make sure that your guests do not make other plans for dinner and bring the appropriate footwear.

Time Line:

The time of the reception is indicated on the second line. It usually reads "immediately following the ceremony". This phrase is not meant to be taken literally. It simply means that the reception will begin in approximately the amount of time it takes to get from the wedding to the reception hall.

The actual time is given when the reception is scheduled to start two hours or more after the ceremony. In this case, the time line reads "at eight o'clock".

Location Line:

The third line gives the name of the facility at which the reception is being held. Its address may be shown on the next line if direction cards are not included and the facility is not well known. If your reception is being held at home, the address is shown. If it is being held at someone else's home, their names and address appear.

City and State Line:

The city and state are included when the ceremony and reception are held in different towns. If the city and state are not shown on the reception cards, it is assumed that the reception is being held in the same town as the ceremony. (The state may be omitted when the towns are different, but are both in the same state.)

Reception Held at Home:

Reception
immediately following the ceremony
307 West Shore Road

Reception Held at Another's Home:

Reception
immediately following the ceremony
at the residence of
Mr. and Mrs. Robert Anthony Dignan
106 Cove Road

Reception Held on a Yacht:

Reception
immediately following the ceremony
aboard the Sea Treasure
Huntington Yacht Club
The Sea Treasure
sails promptly at eight o'clock

Reply Information:

When reply cards are not sent with the invitations, reply request information must appear in the lower left-hand corner of the reception cards.

The first line requests a reply. It may read "The favour of a reply is requested", "R.s.v.p.", "R.S.V.P." or "Please reply". All four are considered proper although there are some regional preferences. For example, in the southern United States, "The favour of a reply is requested" is overwhelmingly popular while the use of "R.s.v.p." is generally frowned upon.

The next two lines give the address to which the replies should be sent. Replies are sent to the person or persons whose names first appear on the invitations, in most cases, the parents of the bride. When the replies are to be sent to somebody else, that person's name appears with the address.

Replies Sent to Bride Instead of Parents:

The favour of a reply is requested
Miss Christina Lee Travis
675 West Neck Road
Huntington, New York 11743

Dress Codes, Children and Gifts:

Appropriate dress has been traditionally indicated by the time of day and the location of the reception. (After six o'clock in the evening is considered formal.) With many of your guests potentially unaware of this point of etiquette, you may find it necessary to indicate appropriate dress on your reception cards. Formal dress is indicated with the words "Black tie". The "B" is always upper case while the "t" is always lower case. This information appears in the lower right-hand corner.

Children of guests are invited simply by including their names on the inside envelopes. (See Wedding Envelopes chapter.) Less simple is how to indicate that children are not invited. While it may be tempting to handle this situation with a corner line reading "No children, please", it is best handled with personal phone calls to family members who may feel entitled to bring their uninvited children with them.

Since it is in poor taste to ask for gifts, it is never appropriate to include information concerning where you are registered. The best way to disseminate this information is by word of mouth.

AT HOME CARDS

At home cards are an effective way to let your family and friends know of your new address. They let people know where you will be living and when you will start residing there. At home cards may be sent with both invitations and announcements, although they are sent much more frequently with announcements. They are not gift solicitations. They simply provide recipients with your address.

When sent with announcements, the bride's and groom's married names appear. When sent with invitations, however, their names are omitted. This is because the bride and groom are not married at the time the invitations are sent so the bride is not yet entitled to use her married name.

Brides who keep their maiden names can use at home cards to convey that information. Brides and grooms do this by showing their names (without titles) on the first two lines followed by the date and their address. This works especially well on announcements since the bride and groom can be presented as "Mr. and Mrs." at the time the announcements are sent.

Sent with Announcements:

Mr. and Mrs. Allen Jay Fannin

233 East 73rd Street
New York, New York 10021

after the first of July

Sent with Invitations:

At home
after the first of July
233 East 73rd Street
New York, New York 10021

Bride Retains Her Maiden Name:

Christina Lee Travis
Andrew Jay Fannin
after the first of July
233 East 73rd Street
New York, New York 10021

Reply Cards and Envelopes:

Wedding invitations were once always responded to with a handwritten note, written on a plain, folded letter sheet. Today, reply cards are used instead.

Reply cards always provide space for the guests' names and response. Most request a reply before a specified date (usually two weeks before the wedding). Requests reading "number of guests" should be avoided as they might encourage some of your guests to invite their own guests.

Reply Cards:

$\mathcal{M}$ _____

_____ *will attend*

The favour of a reply is requested before the twentieth of May

Reply envelopes have the name and address of the person to whom the reply is being sent printed on the front of the envelope.

CEREMONY CARDS

When the main invitations are to the reception, ceremony cards are enclosed with the invitations that are sent to those guests who are also invited to the ceremony. Since they serve as invitations to your wedding ceremony, formal wording is appropriate. The terms "marriage ceremony" and "wedding ceremony" are both correct. Whichever word (marriage or wedding) is used on the reception invitations is repeated on the ceremony cards.

Mr. and Mrs. Paul James Travis
request the honour of your presence
at the marriage ceremony
Saturday, the sixth of June
at six o'clock
Old First Presbyterian Church

or

The honour of your presence
is requested at the wedding ceremony
Saturday, the sixth of June
at six o'clock
Old First Presbyterian Church

DIRECTION AND MAP CARDS

Direction cards give simple and concise directions to your wedding. In order to make them easier to read while driving, they should be printed in a sans-serif (block) lettering style. Map cards are small maps that highlight the routes to your wedding. Direction cards and map cards should be printed on the same quality paper as your invitations. Those furnished by houses of worship and banquet halls and photocopies are not appropriate.

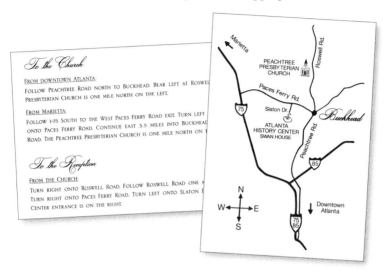

SAVE-THE-DATE CARDS

Also known as hold-the-date cards, these cards are sent to guests who might need to plan for your wedding well in advance of its date. They ask your guests to set aside that date for your wedding and are generally sent three to four months before the wedding. They in no way take the place of an invitation. The actual invitation is sent at a later date, usually four to six weeks before the wedding.

Please save the date of
Saturday, the sixth of June
for the wedding of
Miss Christina Lee Travis

to

Mr. Andrew Jay Fannin
Mr. and Mrs. Paul James Travis

ACCOMMODATION CARDS

Accommodation cards are sent to out-of-town guests who may need to make hotel arrangements. These cards list the names and phone numbers of convenient hotels. If you are paying for your guests' rooms, a notation to that effect is made. If not, you may add a line suggesting that they call the hotel for rates.

Accommodations:

The Anchorage Inn
(516) 555-1234

Huntington Hilton
(516) 555-1212

For rates and reservations, please call

A room for you has been reserved at:

The Anchorage Inn
1550 Mill Dam Road
Huntington, New York

(516) 555-1234

TRANSPORTATION CARDS

When transportation has been arranged for your guests, transportation cards are included with their invitations.

Transportation will be provided
from the ceremony to the reception

Transportation home after the reception
will be provided

PEW CARDS

Pew cards are sent with invitations when guests have been assigned specific pews. They are presented at the ceremony to assist the ushers in efficiently seating your guests in their appropriate pews. The pew number is written by hand, usually in calligraphy, in the space provided.

Please present this card at
Old First Presbyterian Church
Saturday, the sixth of June

Pew number_____

WITHIN THE RIBBON CARDS

Cards reading "Within the ribbon" inform ushers that guests should be seated in special sections identified by a ribbon or a cord.

Within the ribbon

ADMISSION CARDS

Admission cards are used when celebrities or dignitaries want to make sure that only their invited guests attend their weddings. The cards serve as tickets and must be presented at the service in order to gain entry. Formal invitations in which the guests', names are written in can also serve as admission cards.

Please present this card at
Old First Presbyterian Church
Saturday, the sixth of June

Mrs. Edward Cummings
will please present this card at
Old First Presbyterian Church
Saturday, the sixth of June

ASSEMBLING WEDDING INVITATIONS

Before the advent of the post office, invitations were delivered by footmen. Due to the nature of their occupation, their hands were dirty and soiled. So, when they handled correspondence like wedding invitations, the envelopes became soiled as well. To avoid the embarrassment of guests receiving soiled envelopes, invitations were delivered in two envelopes. Upon receipt, the soiled outside envelopes were discarded, and the invitations were presented in their clean inside envelopes. The inside envelopes bore just the names of the recipients. There were no addresses on them as they were already at their intended destinations. They just needed to be distributed to the appropriate party in that household. The custom of mailing wedding invitations in double envelopes endures to this day.

Wedding invitations are assembled in size order. You start with the invitation. The enclosure cards are then stacked on top (not inside). The reception card goes first, placed face-up on top of the invitation. Next is the reply envelope, placed face-down on top of the reception card. The reply card is slipped face-up beneath (not inside) the flap of the reply envelope. If used, the at home card, direction card, accommodation card, and pew card are added in that order. Once the invitation and enclosures are assembled, they are placed into the inside envelope with the folded end of the invitation at the bottom of the envelope. The copy faces the back of the envelope. The way that you can tell if you stuffed an envelope correctly is by removing the invitation with your right hand. If you can read the invitation without turning it, you have inserted it correctly.

Tissues:

Wedding invitations were once engraved with oil-based inks. These inks were slow to dry, so tissue was inserted between the invitations to prevent smudging. Etiquette called for removing the tissues since they were merely packing material. However, many brides, thinking the tissues were ornamentation of some kind, left them in. As more and more brides did this, the etiquette changed and now it is equally proper to send tissued invitations.

Tissues actually serve a new purpose now. The sorting equipment used by the postal service can cause smudging on invitations sent without tissues. So, it might be wise to either use tissues or to ask the postal service to hand-cancel your invitations.

ADDRESSING THE ENVELOPES

As mentioned in the previous section, wedding invitations and announcements are mailed in two envelopes.

Outside Envelopes:

The outside envelope is the mailing envelope. Your guests' names and addresses are handwritten or calligraphed in black ink on the face of the envelopes.

Mr. and Mrs. Adam Smith
1234 Chester Street
Great Barrington,
Massachusetts 56789

Abbreviations:

Abbreviations such as "St." or "Ave." are never used. However, abbreviated titles such as "Mr.", "Mrs." and "Dr." may be used. While "Ms." is too informal to appear on a wedding invitation, it may be used when addressing envelopes.

Return Address:

The sender's return address is engraved or blind embossed on the back flap. Blind embossing is preferred because of the feeling that the first time your guests see the beautiful engraving should be on the invitation. The senders' names do not appear with the return address. Therefore, if you live in an apartment building, you need to include your apartment number. Your apartment number may appear alone on the first line with your street address on line two or following your street address on the same line.

Apartment 12c
307 West Shore Road
Huntington, New York 11743

307 West Shore Road, Apartment 12c
Huntington, New York 11743

Inside Envelopes:

The inside envelope informs its recipients which members of the household are invited to your wedding. Therefore, just the names of those members of the household are written on the inside envelopes. Only surnames and titles are used. If children under eighteen are invited, their given names are written on a second line. Avoid using "and family" as it is ambiguous and may encourage some of your guests to add to your guest list.

Escorts and Guests:

When you would like one of your guests to bring their own guest to your wedding, correct etiquette requires that you call your guest and find out the name and address of the person whom he or she would like to invite. After receiving that information, you then send that person a separate invitation.

If you are unable to obtain that information, you may need to use the terms "and guest" or "and escort". A man brings a guest while a woman is escorted by a man. Therefore, when inviting a man and his guest, use the term "and guest". When inviting a woman and her guest, use either "and escort" or "and guest". "Guest" and "escort" are written entirely with lower case letters.

MARRIED COUPLE

OUTSIDE ENVELOPE   INSIDE ENVELOPE
Mr. and Mrs. Troy Clayton   *Mr. and Mrs. Clayton*

with Children under Eighteen Living at Home:
OUTSIDE ENVELOPE   INSIDE ENVELOPE
Mr. and Mrs. Troy Clayton   *Mr. and Mrs. Clayton*
                                         Marvin and Heather

with Two Daughters over Eighteen Living at Home:

OUTSIDE ENVELOPE	INSIDE ENVELOPE
The Misses Clayton	*The Misses Clayton*

or

Miss Heather Clayton
Miss Mindy Clayton

with Two Sons over Eighteen Living at Home:

OUTSIDE ENVELOPE	INSIDE ENVELOPE
The Messrs. Clayton	*The Messrs. Clayton*

or

Mr. Lawrence Clayton
Mr. Kevin Clayton

with a Son and a Daughter over Eighteen Living at Home:

OUTSIDE ENVELOPE	INSIDE ENVELOPE
Miss Heather Clayton	*Miss Clayton*
Mr. Marvin Clayton	*Mr. Clayton*

in Which Woman Kept Maiden Name:

OUTSIDE ENVELOPE	INSIDE ENVELOPE
Ms. Christine Pritchett	*Ms. Pritchett*
and Mr. Troy Clayton	*and Mr. Clayton*

in Which Man is a Doctor:

OUTSIDE ENVELOPE	INSIDE ENVELOPE
Doctor and Mrs. Troy Clayton	*Doctor and Mrs. Clayton*

in Which Both are Doctors:

OUTSIDE ENVELOPE	INSIDE ENVELOPE
Doctor and Mrs. Troy Clayton	*Doctor and Mrs. Clayton*

or   or

| *The Doctors Clayton* | *The Doctors Clayton* |

or

Doctor Christine Clayton
and Doctor Troy Clayton

in Which Woman is a Doctor:

OUTSIDE ENVELOPE	INSIDE ENVELOPE
Mr. and Mrs. Troy Clayton	*Mr. and Mrs. Clayton*

or   or

Doctor Christine Clayton   *Doctor Clayton*
and Mr. Troy Clayton   *and Mr. Clayton*

in Which Man is a Judge:

OUTSIDE ENVELOPE	INSIDE ENVELOPE
The Honorable and Mrs. Troy Clayton	*Judge and Mrs. Clayton*

in Which Woman is a Judge:

OUTSIDE ENVELOPE	INSIDE ENVELOPE
Mr. and Mrs. Troy Clayton	*Mr. and Mrs. Clayton*
or	or
The Honorable Christine Clayton and Mr. Troy Clayton	*Judge Clayton and Mr. Clayton*

in Which One or Both Members Are Lawyers:

OUTSIDE ENVELOPE	INSIDE ENVELOPE
Mr. and Mrs. Troy Clayton	*Mr. and Mrs. Clayton*

UNMARRIED COUPLE LIVING TOGETHER

OUTSIDE ENVELOPE	INSIDE ENVELOPE
Miss Christine Pritchett	*Miss Pritchett*
Mr. Troy Clayton	*Mr. Clayton*
or	or
Ms. Christine Pritchett	*Ms. Pritchett*
Mr. Troy Clayton	*Mr. Clayton*

DIVORCED WOMAN

OUTSIDE ENVELOPE	INSIDE ENVELOPE
Mrs. Christine Pritchett Clayton	*Mrs. Clayton*
or	or
Ms. Christine Pritchett Clayton	*Ms. Clayton*

Who Has Resumed Using Maiden Name:

OUTSIDE ENVELOPE	INSIDE ENVELOPE
Ms. Christine Pritchett	*Ms. Pritchett*

WIDOW

OUTSIDE ENVELOPE	INSIDE ENVELOPE
Mrs. Troy Clayton	*Mrs. Clayton*

SINGLE WOMAN

OUTSIDE ENVELOPE
Miss Christine Pritchett
or
Ms. Christine Pritchett

INSIDE ENVELOPE
Miss Pritchett
or
Ms. Pritchett

and Date:

OUTSIDE ENVELOPE
Miss Christine Pritchett
or
Ms. Christine Pritchett

INSIDE ENVELOPE
Miss Pritchett and escort
or
Miss Pritchett and guest
or
Ms. Pritchett and escort
or
Ms. Pritchett and guest

SINGLE MAN

OUTSIDE ENVELOPE
Mr. Troy Clayton

INSIDE ENVELOPE
Mr. Clayton

and Date:

OUTSIDE ENVELOPE
Mr. Troy Clayton

INSIDE ENVELOPE
Mr. Clayton and guest

MILITARY TITLES

*Please note that the service designation should always appear on the same line with the name and rank. In the following entries, service designations that appear on separate lines do so to accommodate space limitations.

MARRIED COUPLES

in Which Man Is an Officer:

OUTSIDE ENVELOPE
Colonel and Mrs. Troy Clayton

INSIDE ENVELOPE
Colonel and Mrs. Clayton

in Which Man Is a Noncommissioned Officer or Enlisted Man:

OUTSIDE ENVELOPE
Mr. and Mrs. Troy Clayton

INSIDE ENVELOPE
Mr. and Mrs. Clayton

in Which Man Is a Retired Officer:

OUTSIDE ENVELOPE	INSIDE ENVELOPE
Colonel and Mrs. Troy Clayton	*Colonel and Mrs. Clayton*

in Which Woman Is an Officer:

OUTSIDE ENVELOPE	INSIDE ENVELOPE
Mr. and Mrs. Troy Clayton	*Mr. and Mrs. Clayton*
or	or
Captain Christine Clayton, U.S. Army and Mr. Troy Clayton	*Captain Clayton and Mr. Troy Clayton*

in Which Both Are Officers:

OUTSIDE ENVELOPE	INSIDE ENVELOPE
Colonel and Mrs. Troy Clayton	*Colonel and Mrs. Clayton*
or	or
Captain Christine Clayton, U.S. Army and Colonel Troy Clayton, U.S. Army	*Captain Clayton and Colonel Clayton*

SINGLE WOMAN

Who Is an Officer:

OUTSIDE ENVELOPE	INSIDE ENVELOPE
Captain Christine Pritchett, U.S. Army	*Captain Pritchett*

Who Is a Junior Officer:

OUTSIDE ENVELOPE	INSIDE ENVELOPE
Lieutenant Christine Pritchett, U.S. Army	*Lieutenant Pritchett*

Who Is a Noncommissioned Officer or Enlisted Woman:

OUTSIDE ENVELOPE	INSIDE ENVELOPE
Miss Christine Pritchett	*Miss Pritchett*
or	or
Ms. Christine Pritchett	*Ms. Pritchett*

SINGLE MAN

Who Is an Officer:

OUTSIDE ENVELOPE	INSIDE ENVELOPE
Colonel Troy Clayton, U.S. Army	*Colonel Clayton*

Who Is a Junior Officer:

OUTSIDE ENVELOPE	INSIDE ENVELOPE
Lieutenant Troy Clayton, U.S. Army	*Lieutenant Clayton*

Who Is a Noncommissioned Officer or Enlisted Man:

OUTSIDE ENVELOPE	INSIDE ENVELOPE
Mr. Troy Clayton	*Mr. Clayton*

MAILING WEDDING INVITATIONS
AND ANNOUNCEMENTS:

Wedding invitations are generally mailed four to six weeks before the weddings. For summer or holiday weddings, you may want to mail them eight weeks before your wedding.

Wedding announcements are mailed after the wedding has taken place. While most brides mail their announcements the day after their wedding, announcements may be properly sent up to one year after the wedding.

The size of your invitation or announcement, the number of enclosures, and even the humidity will affect the weight of your invitations. Be sure to have them weighed ahead of time at your local post office in order to determine the postage.

INVITATIONS
TO
SOCIAL OCCASIONS

INTRODUCTION

*I*nvitations to social occasions may be formal, informal, or anything in
between. The formality of your invitations should match the formality
(or informality) of your event. The invitation that you send sets the
tone for your event and helps your guests determine appropriate dress.
Formal events, such as a black tie reception, require a formal invitation
while less formal events, like a cook-out, allow more freedom. Invitations for
formal events are done on white or ecru (ivory or buff) cards, generally in
black ink. Invitations to other events may be done on correspondence cards
with bright colored borders with matching lined envelopes. The lettering may
be fun and frivolous. This is your opportunity to be as creative as your imag-
ination allows.

Your invitations may be engraved or thermographed. Engraving is the
more formal and elegant process while thermography is a little less formal,
and less expensive.

Whether formal or not, the composition of your invitations contains the
same basic elements. In other words, while the rules of etiquette for informal
invitations are not as strict as those for formal invitations, the same information must be included, for example, host, event, date, time, and place.

While it is impossible to include examples of every type of invitation that you might send, you can easily come up with your own wording by looking at the samples provided and substituting your own information for the information in the sample. For example, if you were hosting a dinner dance celebrating your parents' anniversary, you could follow the format below, substituting your names on the invitation line, "dinner dance" for "cocktails and dinner" on the event line and by adding "in honour of ", "the fortieth wedding anniversary of", and your parents' names on the subsequent lines. See Sample #2.

The order in which your information appears is not necessarily dictated by convention. You may wish to afford your guest of honor more distinction. You can do this by moving his name from the body of the invitation to the top. Notice that Samples #1 and #3 have identical information.

In Sample #4, the event is more casual and so is the wording.

As you will see, all four sample invitations have varying degrees of formality yet carry the same basic information. When you compose your invitations follow one of the samples (or create your own format) and simply make sure that you include all of the necessary information.

Sample #1:

Invitation Line	*Mr. and Mrs. Stephen Julian Hameroff*
Request line	*request the pleasure of your company*
Event Line #1	*at a cocktail party*
Event Line #2	*to meet*
Event Line # 3	*Mrs. David Allen Meppen*
Date Line	*Saturday, the fifteenth of June*
Time Line	*at seven o'clock*
Address Line	*The Warwick Hotel*
City and State Line	*Houston, Texas*
Reply Request Line	*The favour of a reply is requested*

Sample #2:

Invitation Line	*Mr. and Mrs. Stephen Julian Hameroff*
Request line	*request the pleasure of your company*
Event Line #1	*at a dinner dance*
Event Line #2	*in honour of*
Event Line # 3	*the fortieth wedding anniversary of*
Event Line #4	*Mr. and Mrs. David Allen Meppen*
Date Line	*Saturday, the fifteenth of June*
Time Line	*at seven o'clock*
Address Line	*The Warwick Hotel*
City and State Line	*Houston, Texas*
Reply Request Line	*The favour of a reply is requested*

Sample #3:

Event Line #2	*To meet*
Event Line # 3	*Mrs. David Allen Meppen*
Invitation Line	*Mr. and Mrs. Stephen Julian Hameroff*
Request line	*request the pleasure of your company*
Event Line #1	*at a cocktail party*
Date Line	*Saturday, the fifteenth of June*
Time Line	*at seven o'clock*
Address Line	*2126 Lazy Lane*
City and State Line	*Houston, Texas*
Reply Request Line	*The favour of a reply is requested*

Sample #4:

Invitation Line	*Debbie and Steve Hameroff*
Request line	*invite you to*
Event Line	*a pool party and barbeque*
Date Line	*Saturday, June 15th*
Time Line	*at 1:00*
Address Line	*2126 Lazy Lane*
City and State Line	*Houston, Texas*
Reply Request Line	*Please reply*

INVITATIONS TO A FORMAL DINNER

Formal dinner invitations are properly engraved on ecru or white letter sheets. Letter sheets are single sheets of paper that fold like a book on the left hand side. (Traditional wedding invitations are done on letter sheets.)

Correspondence cards (flat, heavy, single cards) are occasionally used as well, but they are considered a little less formal.

Black ink is the color of choice for formal invitations, but any conservative ink color will make a tasteful invitation.

The most formal invitations leave a space for your guests' names to be handwritten or calligraphed. (See first sample below.) This format gives special honor to your guests. When wording an invitation to dinner, it is important to remember that guests are invited "at a dinner" or "to a dinner", never "for dinner" unless they are being served as the entree.

Mr. and Mrs. Jeffrey Harris Atkinson

request the pleasure of the company of

Mr. and Mrs. Charles Winn Montgomery

at dinner

Friday, the eighteenth of November

at eight o'clock

922 Club Creek

Grosse Pointe Farms, Michigan

INVITATIONS TO A DINNER TO HONOR A GUEST

Invitations that honor a guest follow the same rules as those for formal dinners. However, the honoree's name is added to the invitations. This may be done in the body of the invitations or at the top. You doubly distinguish your honored guest by placing his or her name at the top of the invitations. The use of "honor" and "honour" are equally correct.

IN HONOUR OF

ADMIRAL WILLIAM STANTON TAGG

MR. AND MRS. ARTHUR DAVID LINCOLN

REQUEST THE PLEASURE OF YOUR COMPANY

AT DINNER

THURSDAY, THE TENTH OF OCTOBER

AT EIGHT O'CLOCK

1825 SYCAMORE LANE

CHARLESTON, SOUTH CAROLINA

INVITATIONS TO MEET A GUEST

Invitations to meet a guest are extended when the hosts wish to introduce somebody to their friends, family, and associates. The party might be held to meet a celebrity, someone new in the area, or, perhaps, your daughter's fiancé. The guidelines follow those for invitations to honor a guest.

To Meet

Miss Kimberly Ann Keleher

Mr. and Mrs. Peter Thomas Madison

request the pleasure of your company

for cocktails

Wednesday, the second of April

at seven o'clock

4209 Granada Boulevard

Coral Gables, Florida

GOVERNMENT AND DIPLOMATIC INVITATIONS

Invitations issued by government officials are engraved in black ink on ecru or white letter sheets or correspondence cards. The correct forms of address for United States government officials are included in the appendix. Please note that government officials do not properly refer to themselves as "The Honorable". That appellation is properly used only when they are addressed by others, such as when an envelope is addressed to them.

Protocol demands that events hosted by, or in honor of, a foreign dignitary require properly worded invitations. If the event is in honor of a dignitary, "In honour of" or "In honor of" appears at the top of the invitations. The dignitaries title must be properly presented. As etiquette varies so much from one country to the next, the best way to make sure that your diplomatic invitations are correct is to check with the protocol office of the appropriate consulate.

To have the honour to meet
Their Majesties
The King and Queen of Siam

The Governor of Hawaii
requests the pleasure of your company
at luncheon
at Washington Place
Thursday, September seventeenth
at one o'clock

PARTY INVITATIONS

Invitations to informal parties reflect the nature of the event. They may be festive, lighthearted or conservative. Sample invitations are displayed below. By starting with these samples, you can create distinctive invitations for any event.

Please join us at home for
Cocktails, Dinner and Music
to celebrate Jeremy's successful audition
with the Spokane Philharmonic Orchestra
Saturday, the tenth of August
at seven o'clock

Mr. and Mrs. McCutcheon

An Evening Under the Stars
Please join us for
Cocktails, Dinner and Dancing
Friday, the eleventh of September
at seven o'clock
Bayview Yacht Club
Tampa, Florida

Lilyan and Robert Stowe

Nina and Terrence McCarty
request the pleasure of your company
at an Alfresco Dinner Party
Saturday, the twentieth of July
half after seven o'clock
Long Point Cottage
Kiawah Island

DANCE INVITATIONS

Dance invitations follow the same format as formal invitations. The event may be mentioned in the body of the invitation by using either "at a small dance" or "at a ball". It may also be mentioned in the lower right-hand corner simply as "Dancing".

Mr. and Mrs. Stephen James McGee
request the pleasure of your company
at a small dance
Saturday , the sixth of November
at ten o'clock in the evening
The Waldorf-Astoria
New York City

R.s.v.p.
1040 Fifth Avenue
New York, New York 10021

Mr. and Mrs. Stephen James McGee
request the pleasure of your company
Saturday , the sixth of November
at ten o'clock in the evening
The Waldorf-Astoria
New York City

R.s.v.p.
1040 Fifth Avenue
New York, New York 10021   Dancing

LUNCHEON INVITATIONS

Invitations to a luncheon may be formal or informal depending on the nature of the event. If formal, black ink engraved on white or ecru cards is preferred.

In honour of

DR. HILTON GARRISON CRENSHAW

MR. AND MRS. JAMES GORDON HARRIS

REQUEST THE PLEASURE OF YOUR COMPANY

AT LUNCHEON

TUESDAY, THE TENTH OF MAY

AT TWELVE O'CLOCK

THE BROWN PALACE HOTEL

DENVER, COLORADO

Ellen Gardiner and Allison Tennant
invite you to a
Bridal Shower Luncheon
in honour of
Caryn Elisabeth Swann
Sunday afternoon, April sixteenth
at one o'clock
Ten Candlewood Lane
Mystic, Connecticut

INVITATIONS TO A TEA

Invitations to a tea are usually engraved in black ink on a white or ecru card. The phrases, "At Home" or "at a tea" are used on invitations to an afternoon tea.

Mrs. John Leland Kensington

At Home

Tuesday, the thirteenth of September

from four until six o'clock

1776 Stone Drive

Birmingham, Alabama

MRS. JOHN LELAND KENSINGTON

REQUESTS THE PLEASURE OF YOUR COMPANY

AT A TEA

TUESDAY, THE THIRTEENTH OF SEPTEMBER

FROM FOUR UNTIL SIX O'CLOCK

1776 STONE DRIVE

BIRMINGHAM, ALABAMA

WEDDING ANNIVERSARIES

Invitations to an event celebrating a wedding anniversary may be extended by the children of the couple, friends of the couple, or by the couple themselves. The year in which they were married and the anniversary year may appear at the top of the invitations. While it is not strictly proper for couples to use a joint monogram, many do when issuing invitations to a party celebrating a wedding anniversary. When doing so, the larger center initial represents the couple's surname. The initial on the left represents the wife's initial. The one on the right is the husband's.

The invitations may be engraved in gold for a fiftieth wedding anniversary, ruby red for a fortieth, or silver for a twenty-fifth. Since some of your guests might have difficulty reading metallic inks, you might consider engraving the dates in gold or silver and the body of the invitation in black.

Since many couples may not feel comfortable receiving gifts, a line in the lower right-hand corner reading, "No gifts, please" may be included. Other options include a separate card reading, "Your presence is the only gift that we request" or even a phone call.

1983 ◆ 2008

Mr. and Mrs. David Leighton Essex

request the pleasure of your company

at a dance to celebrate their

Twenty-fifth Wedding Anniversary

Saturday, the seventh of June

at eight o'clock

The Diamond Club

24 Tate Street

Chicago

Please reply
(312) 555-1212

BRIDAL SHOWER INVITATIONS

The modern bridal shower is a throwback to the days when a bride brought her dowry to the marriage. Provided by her father, the dowry made her more attractive to potential husbands and gave the newly married couple the material goods and finances needed to help them start their new lives together. Modern bridal showers attended by family and friends, allow today's brides and grooms the basic necessities to furnish their new homes.

Invitations to bridal showers are usually fun and informal. Bridal showers are hosted by one or more of the bride's friends, never by a member of her family. The hostesses' names appear at the top of the invitations.

Many showers have themes such as linens, kitchen, and lingerie. For older brides, themes might include golf, tennis, garden, and travel. When a shower has a theme, the theme is mentioned in either the lower left- or lower right-hand corner.

Susan Marie Neely

requests the pleasure of your company

at a Bridal Shower in honor of

Katherine Anne Carlson

Thursday, the fifteenth of May

at seven o'clock

17 Park Street

Andover, Massachusetts

Linens

Susan Neely

cordially invites you

to a Bridal Shower

in honor of

Kathy Carlson

on Thursday, May fifteenth

at seven o'clock

17 Park Street

Andover, Massachusetts

BABY SHOWER INVITATIONS

The guidelines for baby showers are similar to those for bridal showers.

Janet Russell
cordially invites you
to a surprise baby shower in honour of
Margaret McQuinn
on Thursday, November 7th at 7 o'clock
14 Briarwood Court
Philadelphia, Pennsylvania

COMMENCEMENT INVITATIONS

Commencement invitations are sent on behalf of a school or university, inviting family and friends to the graduation ceremony.

THE FACULTY AND GRADUATING CLASS

OF

SAINT MICHAEL'S ACADEMY

REQUEST THE PLEASURE OF YOUR COMPANY AT THEIR

ANNUAL COMMENCEMENT EXERCISES

SATURDAY, THE TWENTIETH OF JUNE

NINETEEN HUNDRED AND NINETY-FIVE

AT THREE O'CLOCK

ALUMNI AUDITORIUM

SHAKER HEIGHTS, OHIO

DEBUTANTE INVITATIONS

Young women are traditionally presented to society at a debutante ball. They may be presented at a private ball or along with other young women at a mass ball, or cotillion. Due to the expenses involved, group balls are much more prevalent.

There are a series of events leading up to the debutante ball including dinners, teas, tea-dances, and small dances.

Dinner:

A debutante dinner party honors the debutante and is given during the social season preceding the debutante ball.

Mr. and Mrs. Paul Thomas Kroeger

request the pleasure of your company

at dinner

in honour of their daughter

Miss Whitney Warner Kroeger

Friday, the fifth of December

at seven o'clock

377 Parkside Lane

Scarsdale, New York

R.s.v.p.   *Dancing*

Tea:

Teas are given in the late afternoon. The phrase "At Home" is used to indicate that the invitation is for a tea. The tea is usually held for women of the debutante's mother's generation and older.

> *Mr. and Mrs. Paul Thomas Kroeger*
>
> *Miss Whitney Warner Kroeger*
>
> *At Home*
>
> *Saturday, the sixth of November*
>
> *at five o'clock*

Tea Dance:

The tea-dance is held for the debutante's friends.

> *Mr. and Mrs. Paul Thomas Kroeger*
>
> *Miss Whitney Warner Kroeger*
>
> *At Home*
>
> *Saturday, the sixth of November*
>
> *at five o'clock*
>
> *Dancing*

Small Dance:

A small dance is a dance of any size, large or small, given to honor the debutante.

Mr. and Mrs. Paul Thomas Kroeger
request the pleasure of your company
at a small dance in honour of
Miss Whitney Warner Kroeger
Saturday, the second of December
at nine o'clock
Sleepy Hollow Country Club
Scarborough, New York

Cotillion:

A cotillion is a group ball during which a number of young women debut.

The Governors of Sleepy Hollow
request the pleasure of the company of
Miss April Lee Fairbanks
at a ball
Saturday, the ninth of December
at nine o'clock
Sleepy Hollow Country Club
Scarborough, New York

BAR/BAT MITZVAH INVITATIONS

"Bar mitzvah" and "bat mitzvah" mean son of the commandments and daughter of the commandments respectively. A bar mitzvah is a boy who, upon reaching the age of thirteen, has attained the age of religious duty and responsibility. Bar mitzvah is also the name of the religious ceremony that is performed to recognize the attainment of religious maturity. A bat mitzvah (Hebrew) or a bas mitzvah (Yiddish) is a girl who achieves religious maturity, also at the age of thirteen. Bat mitzvah and bas mitzvah also refer to the ceremony.

While there is no standard etiquette for a bar or bat mitzvah invitation, it should be remembered that these are sacred religious ceremonies. The invitations should be tasteful and conservative in keeping with the solemnity of the occasion.

Mr. and Mrs. Samuel Greenberg
request the honour of your presence
at the Bar Mitzvah of their son
Steven
Saturday, the seventh of April
at ten o'clock
Temple Beth Israel
Palm Beach

Luncheon following the services

FILL-IN INVITATIONS

Fill-in or skeleton invitations are personalized invitations that leave blank the areas for some of the information, such as the event, the date, and the time. They are usually ordered in large quantities and are used as the occasion arises. The "missing" information is filled in by hand.

Fill-in invitations may also be purchased over-the-counter without any personalization.

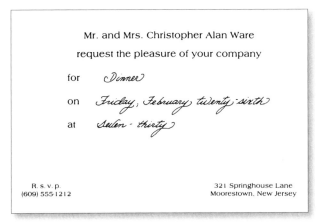

Mr. and Mrs. Christopher Alan Ware
request the pleasure of your company

for   *Dinner*

on   *Friday, February, twenty-sixth*

at   *Seven - thirty*

R. s. v. p.
(609) 555-1212

321 Springhouse Lane
Moorestown, New Jersey

REMINDER CARDS

Reminder cards confirm information regarding your event. You may want to send them when you have sent invitations well in advance of an event or when an invitation was extended by phone. You may also send them, as a courtesy, to the guest of honor.

Your reminder cards may be personalized for either a specific event or as non-specific fill-ins. Reminder cards can also be purchased over the counter without personalization. Invitations with the words "To Remind" written on them can also be used as reminder cards. Since a reminder card does not require a reply, the reply request information should not appear.

Reminder cards are sent so that they arrive one week before the event.

This is to remind you that

Mr. and Mrs. Taylor Ashton Wells

expect you for dinner

Friday, the twenty-first of January

at eight o'clock

1220 Alta Loma Road

Los Angeles, California

SAVE THE-DATE CARDS

Also known as hold-the-date cards, these cards are sent to guests who might need advance notification of an event so that they can make special arrangements. They are generally sent when an event is being held at a time when guests might otherwise make plans, such as holiday weekends. Save-the-date cards ask your guests to set aside that date for your event and are generally sent three to four months before the event. They do not take the place of invitations. The actual invitations are sent at a later date, usually four to six weeks before the event.

> Please hold the date of
>
> Saturday, the third of March
>
> for a dinner in honour of
>
> Dr. Linda Evelyn Berthume
>
>
> Mr. and Mrs. Winthrop Phillip Byerly

FORMAL REPLIES

Replies to formal invitations should be sent within three days of your receipt of the invitation or before the reply date given on the invitation. They are handwritten in black ink on the first page of ecru or white letter sheets. (Letter sheets have a fold along the left-hand side, like formal wedding invitations.) The replies are written in the third person and follow the format of the invitation. They are sent to the persons issuing the invitation. If more than one name or couple are listed, the replies are sent to whomever is listed first on the invitation.

Acceptances repeat the date and time. Regrets repeat just the date and may include a brief reason for not being able to accept. Mentioning the event is optional. If you do mention the event use "on" before the date. Otherwise, use "for".

Invitations from the White House always take precedence over other invitations. The only acceptable excuses for refusing invitations from the White House are illness, a death in the family, a wedding in the family, and being out of the country.

Acceptance:

> Mr. and Mrs. Taylor Randall Carr
> accept with pleasure
> the kind invitation of
> Mr. and Mrs. Travis
> to dinner
> on Saturday, the sixth of June
> at six o'clock

Regret:

> Mr. and Mrs. Taylor Randall Carr
> regret that because of a previous commitment
> they are unable to accept
> the kind invitation of
> Mr. and Mrs. Travis
> for Saturday, the sixth of June

Acceptance with Children:

> Mr. and Mrs. Taylor Randall Carr
> Esta, Janice, Barbara
> accept with pleasure

Wife Accepts, Husband Regrets:

> Mrs. Taylor Randall Carr
> accepts with pleasure
> the kind invitation of
> Mr. and Mrs. Travis
> to dinner
> for Saturday, the sixth of June
> at six o'clock
> Mr. Taylor Randall Carr
> regrets that he is unable to accept
> due to a previous commitment

INFORMAL REPLIES

Replies to informal invitations should be as formal or informal as the closeness of your relationship to the host or hostess dictates. For example, a reply sent to your mother should be a lot less formal than one sent to somebody you just met. If you are sending a regret, you should briefly state the reason. Replies should be made within three days and can be written on informals, fold-over notes, or even calling cards. If you use your calling cards, be sure to send them in a an envelope that is large enough to mail. The smallest allowable mailing envelope measures 3 1/2" x 5".

Acceptance:

Mr. and Mrs. Taylor Randall Carr
accept with pleasure
the kind invitation of
Mr. and Mrs. Bolton
for Saturday, the sixth of June
at six o'clock

Regret:

Mr. and Mrs. Taylor Randall Carr
regret that because of a previous engagement
they are unable to accept
the kind invitation of
Mr. and Mrs. Travis
for Saturday, the sixth of June

Fold-over notes:

Mr. and Mrs. Jay Albert Greschner
accept with pleasure
the kind invitation of
Mr. and Mrs. Kimbrough
to dinner
on Friday, the third of December
at seven o'clock

Informals:

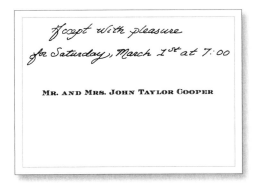

Calling Cards:

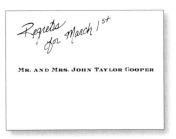

FILLING IN REPLY CARDS

Reply cards are sent with invitations in order to give recipients an easy and convenient way to respond. They should be returned promptly. Your name, preceded by your title is written in following the "M" in the space provided (that is what the "M" is for). If you will be attending the event, the space between "will" and "attend" is left blank. If you will not be attending, write "not" in that space.

BEYOND THE INVITATION

Whether you are entertaining at home, at your club, or in a restaurant, you can enhance the elegance of your event by using menu cards, place cards, table cards, and escort cards.

Menu Cards:

Menu cards can add a nice flourish to your dinner parties. Your special event is made even more special and memorable when you add menu cards to your table settings. Menu cards are white or ecru cards that are generally trimmed in gold or silver. They may be handwritten or printed. Your monogram or your company's logo may be engraved at the top of the cards. You may use a motif instead, such as a scallop shell for a seafood dinner or a cornucopia for a Thanksgiving feast. The menu is listed in the center of the card. The wines are listed to the left alongside their corresponding course. One card is usually shared by two guests although it is entirely appropriate to place one at each guest's place.

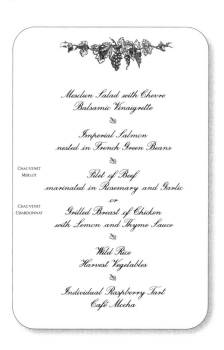

Place Cards:

Place cards are small white or ecru cards that are generally trimmed in gold or silver. They are placed at the table to identify seating arrangements. Folded place cards, also known as tent cards, stand on their own, while flat cards may be used in holders appropriate to the table setting or simply set against the water glass. Like menu cards, place cards may be embellished with your monogram or corporate logo, or with an appropriate motif. Your place cards should always match your menu cards. For example, if your menu cards are engraved with your monogram, your place cards should be engraved with it too.

Your guest's title and surname are written on the card.

Table Cards:

Table cards and envelopes are helpful for small receptions and essential for large ones. Placed on a table outside the reception hall, they direct your guests to their respective tables. Your guests' names are written on the front of the envelope. Their surname, preceded by their titles, are used. If you have more than one guest with the same surname, a first name is added. Their table number is written on the card inside.

SOCIAL ANNOUNCEMENTS, GREETING CARDS AND SOCIAL CORRESPONDENCE

BIRTH ANNOUNCEMENTS

When a child is born, it is customary to send announcements heralding the event. Your choice of birth announcements should reflect your personality. They can be formal and traditional, or less formal and more imaginative.

The most traditional birth announcements are small cards that are attached to larger cards with a pink or blue ribbon. Other traditional announcements may be simple flat cards with a standard format with formal wording.

Less formal announcements can run the gamut from an adorable photo to an imprint of the baby's foot.

The titles "Mr. and Mrs." are used on the most formal announcements, but are dropped on less formal ones. A mother who uses her maiden name has her name appear on the line above the father's name. She does not use a title.

Jordan Elizabeth Spencer

Seven pounds, fourteen ounces   May 3, 2002

Mr. and Mrs. James Ryan Spencer

We are delighted to announce
the birth of our daughter
Kristin Curtis Overbaugh
July 9, 2002

Patricia and Richard Overbaugh

She's cute as a bug!

Twins:

Casey Doyle	Matthew Cory
May 27, 2002	May 27, 2002
5 lbs. 3 ozs.	5 lbs. 7 ozs.

Mr. and Mrs. Charles Hunt Kittredge

ADOPTION ANNOUNCEMENTS

Adoption announcements have the same look and format as birth announcements, but contain additional information. They typically include both the date of birth and the date on which the child was brought home. Sometimes the word "arrived" is used instead of "adopted" as the adoption might not have been finalized before the arrival date. Many parents send adoption announcements as soon as they bring their child home while others wait until the adoption has been legally finalized. If the adoption involves a name change (as with an older child), the announcements generally mention the change.

Mr. and Mrs. Donald Edward Chafee

take pleasure in announcing that

Jennifer Sue Foley

has been adopted as their daughter

and will hereafter be known as

Jennifer Sue Chafee

February 16th, 2003   *April 27th, 2003*

Mr. and Mrs. Robert Thomas Farley

are happy to announce that

Patrick Ryan

joined their family

at five days of age

July 9, 2003

CHRISTENING INVITATIONS

Christening and baptismal invitations are usually very informal. They may be printed in a standard format, engraved in the format of a personal note, or handwritten.

Mr. and Mrs. James Patrick Smith
invite you
to the christening of their daughter
Stephanie
Sunday, the nineteenth of September
at eleven o'clock
Church of Saint Joseph
Seattle, Washington

Reception to follow at home

Stephanie will be christened on Sunday, the nineteenth of September at eleven o'clock at the Church of Saint Joseph. Please join us for this special occasion and for a small luncheon at our home after the service.

Denise and Jim Smith

MR. AND MRS. ANDREW LEIGHTON
REQUEST THE HONOUR OF YOUR PRESENCE
AT THE CHRISTENING OF THEIR DAUGHTER

Lindsay Alexandra

ON SUNDAY, THE SIXTEENTH OF JUNE
AT ELEVEN O'CLOCK
SAINT PATRICK'S CHURCH
WILLIAMSTOWN, MASSACHUSETTS

CHANGE OF NAME ANNOUNCEMENTS

People who legally change their names because of divorce or other reasons may let others know by sending an announcement.

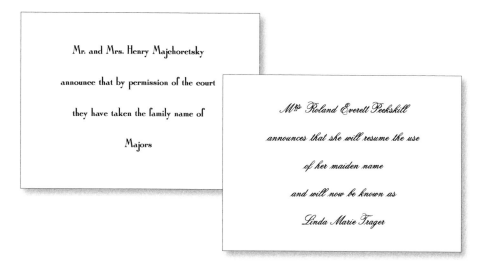

Mr. and Mrs. Henry Majchoretsky

announce that by permission of the court

they have taken the family name of

Majors

Mrs. Roland Everett Peekskill

announces that she will resume the use

of her maiden name

and will now be known as

Linda Marie Trager

CHANGE OF ADDRESS ANNOUNCEMENTS

Change of address announcements are sent to inform family and friends of your new address, phone number and email address.

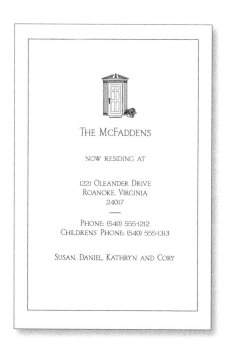

THE McFADDENS

NOW RESIDING AT

1221 OLEANDER DRIVE
ROANOKE, VIRGINIA
24017
—
PHONE: (540) 555-1212
CHILDRENS' PHONE: (540) 555-1313

SUSAN, DANIEL, KATHRYN AND CORY

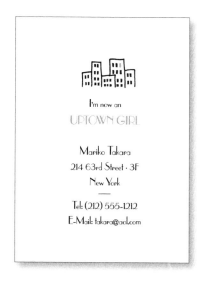

I'm now an
UPTOWN GIRL

Mariko Takara
214 63rd Street · 3F
New York
—
Tel: (212) 555-1212
E-Mail: takara@aol.com

HOLIDAY GREETING CARDS

Individuals, families, and businesses send holiday greeting cards toward the end of the year. While most are sent in December to coincide with Christmas and Chanukah, some are sent in November, usually by businesses, to coincide with Thanksgiving. Holiday cards may express either a generic season's greeting or a religious sentiment. Businesses should stick to a generic message.

Most holiday cards display a seasonal or religious scene on the front of the card with a message inside. Many families use a photo enclosure card which has a photograph of the entire family, just the children, or even the family dog on the front of the card.

Your holiday cards may be personalized by adding your name or your company's name to the sentiment. Cards sent by a couple show the couple's first names followed by their surname. The woman's name appears first. Couples that do not share the same surname list their names on separate lines. Again, the woman's name appears first. Children's names may appear in age order (older to younger) on the same line together with their parents' names or separately on a second line.

Married Couple:	Jeanette and Scott Robison
	or
	Mr. and Mrs. Scott Robison
Couple with Different Surnames:	Jeanette Baker
	Scott Robison
Children's Names:	Jeanette, Scott, Mindy and Tina Robison
	or
	Jeanette and Scott Robison
	Mindy and Tina

Merry Christmas
                                        and a
                                   Happy New Year

                                  Season's Greetings
                                        and
                            Best Wishes for the New Year

                              Wishing you joy and happiness
                                during this holiday season
                              and throughout the New Year

                              Wishing you a joyous Christmas
                                  with health and happiness
                                 through the coming year

                                     May you find
                               health, happiness and peace
                                during this Holiday Season
                               and through the coming year

ROSH HASHANAH CARDS

Cards celebrating the Jewish New Year are sent early enough to arrive before the holiday. Like other holiday cards, they may be sent by individuals, families, or on behalf of corporations.

Your Rosh Hashanah cards may be personalized by adding your name or your company's name to the sentiment. Cards sent by a couple show the couple's first names followed by their surname. The woman's name appears first. Couples that do not share the same surname list their names on separate lines. Again, the woman's name appears first. Children's names may appear in age order (older to younger) on the same line together with their parents' names or separately on a second line.

Married Couple: Judy and Bob Nishman

Couple with Different Surnames: Judy Goldstein
                                       Bob Nishman

Children's Names:	Judy, Bob, Steven, and Bill, Nishman
or	Judy and Bob Nishman
	Steven and Bill

Sample Greetings:	All good wishes
	for health and happiness
	through the coming year
	May the coming
	New Year
	bring you health and happiness

THANK-YOU NOTES

Your appreciation of a gift should be acknowledged as soon after its receipt as possible. Your appreciation seems much more sincere when it is expressed promptly. Notes should be sent to thank someone for sending a gift, having you as a guest for dinner, or for any small favor. If you are not sure whether or not a thank-you note is called for, send one anyway. A note of appreciation is always welcome.

Thank-you notes are generally written on either a small fold-over note or on a correspondence card.

The message is usually brief and generally consists of five parts:

The Greeting:

Dear Barbara,

An appreciation of the gift or favor:

Thank you for the beautiful, hand-carved walking stick.

Mention how useful it will be:

It's already a reliable companion on my daily constitutional.

Suggest a future meeting:

I hope you'll find time to join me for a walk.

Closing:

Love,
Dad

INVITATIONS TO A MEMORIAL SERVICE

A memorial service is given in memory of the deceased. It may be given any time after the burial or cremation. The invitations are formal: black ink on an ecru or white card or letter sheet.

1923   2005

In memoriam

John Alexander Holmes

The honour of your presence
is requested at a memorial service
Wednesday, the twenty-first of January
at seven o'clock
First Methodist Church
Grove City, Pennsylvania

CONDOLENCE NOTES

Condolence notes are letters of sympathy sent to the family of the deceased. They should be sent on a timely basis and should contain sincere expressions of sympathy. Since condolence notes are sent at a difficult time for the family, they should be brief. They should contain personal praise of the deceased and, if appropriate, mention how life was enriched because of him or her. It is always appropriate to end with an offer to be of service to the family.

Dear Tom,

I was so sorry to hear about your father's death. I'll always remember playing ball with him in your backyard and his teaching us to always give our best. I'll miss him greatly.

If there is anything I can do, please let me know.

Sincerely,
Rick

Dear James,

Michael and I are deeply saddened by Melissa's death. Good friends are hard to come by and Melissa was the best. We will always miss her friendship and love.

Please call us if there is anything you need. We're always available.

Love,
Paula

Dear Mrs. Schwartzman,

We were all surprised and saddened by your husband's death. Working for him was a pleasure for all of us. His door was always open to us whenever we had a question or a problem. Coming to work will be a little bit harder for us now.

We hope you will still stop by and visit us when you're in the city.

Sincerely,
Susan Miller

SYMPATHY ACKNOWLEDGMENTS

Sympathy acknowledgments are handwritten notes of appreciation sent to family, friends, and business associates who expressed their condolences. They may be engraved when sent to people who are not known personally by the family or when an overwhelming number of acknowledgments need to be sent. A personal message may always be added to engraved acknowledgments.

Ecru or white cards are generally used for sympathy acknowledgments. They may be plain or bordered in black. At one time, the width of the border signified the sender's closeness to the deceased.

Mrs. Timothy Warren Chandler
wishes to express her appreciation
and sincere thanks
for your kind expression
of sympathy

CALLING CARDS

The History of Calling Cards:

In Europe, the first known use of a calling card occurred in Italy during the latter part of the sixteenth century. The custom spread to France, Great Britain, and eventually the United States.

Calling cards were originally made for the nobility to hand to a footman when paying a call or to leave at the home when the person called upon was absent. Their use was popularized during the reign of Louis XVI when the custom developed in France to use them when paying New Year's calls.

Calligraphers made the early calling cards, which bore the name of the individual and his hereditary titles. The cards were further embellished with borders, floral designs, and other ornamentations. Early in the nineteenth century, these embellishments were abandoned in favor of a fine card on which only the individual's name appeared.

When making a social call, you leave a calling card for each adult on whom you are calling, never, however, exceeding three cards. A man may call on a husband and wife, in which case he leaves two cards. A woman may only call on another woman, so she leaves only one card. You may turn down the corner of your card to signify that it is intended for all the ladies of the house.

Calling cards are still occasionally used for their original purpose, but are now more often used as gift enclosures. The traditional way to personalize a gift enclosure card is by drawing a line through the imprinted name and writing a brief message with your signature.

Calling cards are available in several sizes. Each size indicates male or female, married or single. The following sizes are the traditional sizes used by individuals and couples.

Child	2 1/4" x 1 3/8"
Single Woman	2 7/8" x 2"
Married Woman	3 1/8" x 2 1/4"
Man	3 3/8" x 1 1/2" or
	3 1/2" x 2"
Married Couple	3 3/8" x 2 1/2"

CALLING CARDS FOR MEN

Men's Cards:

A man's full name, preceded by his title, is always used. His middle name is always spelled out, never abbreviated. While "Mr." is always abbreviated, other titles, such as "Doctor" and "Colonel", are spelled out. Suffixes, such as "junior", may follow the name. A man is a junior when he shares the same name as his father. He uses junior until his father passes away. Then, he drops it from his name. If, however, his father were a well-known figure, he would continue to use "junior" to avoid any confusion. It may appear in its abbreviated form as "Jr." or, when space permits, spelled out as "junior". When abbreviated, the "J" is capitalized. When spelled out, the "j" is lower case.

A man uses "II" when he is named after an older relative other than his father. "III" is used when a man is named after somebody who uses "junior" or "II". They are usually preceded by a comma, although some men omit the comma. Traditionally, both formats are correct.

Mr. Griffen Alexander Greylock

Mr. Griffen Alexander Greylock, junior

Mr. Griffen Alexander Greylock, Jr.

Mr. Griffen Alexander Greylock, III

Boy's Cards:

A title does not precede the name of a boy under the age of eighteen.

Thomas Arthur Hancock

CALLING CARDS FOR WOMEN

Married Women:

A married woman uses her husband's full name, preceded by "Mrs." Her husband's middle name is always included and is never replaced by his middle initial. If her husband's name is followed by a suffix, such as "Jr.", that suffix appears on her calling cards as well.

Mrs. Harrison Raiford Booth

Mrs. Harrison Raiford Booth, Jr.

Widows:

A widow continues to use her husband's name on her calling cards. If her son is a junior who has dropped the "Jr." from his name, she adds the suffix, "senior" to distinguish herself from her daughter-in-law. "Senior" may be spelled out with a lower case "s" or abbreviated with a capital "S".

Mrs. Harrison Raiford Booth

Mrs. Harrison Raiford Booth, senior

Mrs. Harrison Raiford Booth, Sr.

Divorced Women:

A divorced woman uses her first name, maiden name, and married name, preceded by "Mrs." She may also use her first, maiden, and married names without a title.

Mrs. Lydia Renner Booth

Lydia Renner Booth

A divorced woman who resumed the use of her maiden name uses her first name, middle name, and last name, without a title.

Lydia Anne Renner

The Use of "Ms.":

"Ms." does not properly appear on calling cards. If a woman feels uncomfortable using "Miss" or "Mrs.", she may omit her title.

Single Woman:

A single woman typically uses her first name, middle name, and last name, preceded by "Miss". She may also omit her title.

Miss Lydia Anne Renner

Lydia Anne Renner

Husband and Wife:

A calling card used jointly by a husband and wife has "Mr. and Mrs." followed by the husband's first name, middle name, and last name. His middle name is always spelled out, never abbreviated. If the husband has a title other than "Mr." that title is used instead. Titles other than "Mr." and "Mrs." should not be abbreviated. When a name is too long to fit on a calling card, it is preferable to omit the middle name rather than to abbreviate a title or use an initial.

Mr. and Mrs. Harrison Raiford Booth

The Reverend and Mrs. Harrison Booth

Medical Doctors:

Physicians, surgeons, and dentists use the prefix "Doctor" or "Dr." on their calling cards. Professional degrees, however, should not appear on cards for social use.

A single woman who is a medical doctor or a married woman who has retained the use of her maiden name or who uses a professional name uses her first name, middle name, and last name, preceded by "Doctor" or "Dr.".

A married woman who is a doctor traditionally uses her husband's first name, middle name, and last name, preceded by "Mrs.". Today, she may instead choose to use her first name, maiden name, and married name, preceded by "Doctor" or "Dr.".

Man: Doctor Jeffrey Allen Glenwood

                       Dr. Jeffrey Allen Glenwood

Single Woman: Doctor Leslie Jean Carpenter

                       Dr. Leslie Jean Carpenter

Married Woman: Mrs. Jeffrey Allen Glenwood

                       Doctor Leslie Carpenter Glenwood

                       Dr. Leslie Allen Glenwood

University and College Titles:

Calling cards for general social use for college and university faculty members show no academic titles or degrees. However, calling cards intended for college and university use do show academic titles. The titles are never abbreviated. If there is not enough room on the card due to a long name and title, the middle name may be abbreviated. Letters indicating advanced degrees do not appear.

General Social Use: Mr. Gregory Winston Hughes

College and University Use: Doctor Gregory Winston Hughes

Clergy:

Members of the clergy use their full names preceded by their title on their calling cards. Titles are never abbreviated. The middle name may be omitted if there is not enough space on the card. No initials indicating divinity degrees appear on the card.

Rabbi Nathan Weisman

The Reverend John Kenneth Rhoads

FORMS
OF
ADDRESS

THE PRESIDENT OF THE UNITED STATES

SALUTATION: Dear Mr. (Madam) President,
CLOSING: Most respectfully yours,
INVITATION, MAN: The President and Mrs. Washington
            WOMAN: The President and Mr. Washington
SOCIAL ENVELOPE, MAN: The President and Mrs. Washington
                WOMAN: The President and Mr. Washington
OFFICIAL ENVELOPE: The President
                The White House
                Washington, D.C. 20500

FORMER PRESIDENT OF THE UNITED STATES

SALUTATION: Dear Mr. (Mrs.) Jefferson,
CLOSING: Sincerely yours,
INVITATION: Mr. and Mrs. Thomas Jefferson
SOCIAL ENVELOPE, MAN: The Honorable Thomas Jefferson
                    and Mrs. Jefferson
            WOMAN: The Honorable Joan Jefferson
                    and Mr. Jefferson
OFFICIAL ENVELOPE: The Honorable Thomas Jefferson

THE VICE PRESIDENT OF THE UNITED STATES

SALUTATION: Dear Mr. (Madam) Vice President,
CLOSING: Sincerely yours,
INVITATION, MAN: The Vice President and Mrs. Adams
          WOMAN: The Vice President and Mr. Adams
SOCIAL ENVELOPE, MAN: The Vice President and Mrs. Adams
          WOMAN: The Vice President and Mr. Adams
OFFICIAL ENVELOPE: The Vice President
                   United States Senate
                   Washington, D.C. 20510

CABINET MEMBER

SALUTATION: Dear Mr. (Madam) Secretary,
CLOSING: Sincerely yours,
INVITATION, MAN: The Secretary of State and Mrs. Novak
          WOMAN: The Secretary of State and Mr. Novak
SOCIAL ENVELOPE, MAN: The Secretary of State and Mrs. Novak
          WOMAN: The Secretary of State and Mr. Novak
OFFICIAL ENVELOPE: The Honorable William Novak
                   Secretary of State
                   Washington, D.C. 20520

ATTORNEY GENERAL

SALUTATION: Dear Mr. (Madam) Attorney General,
CLOSING: Sincerely yours,
INVITATION, MAN: The Attorney General and Mrs. Sharrer
          WOMAN: The Attorney General and Mr. Sharrer
SOCIAL ENVELOPE, MAN: The Attorney General and Mrs. Sharrer
          WOMAN: The Attorney General and Mr. Sharrer
OFFICIAL ENVELOPE: The Honorable Robert Sharrer
                   Attorney General
                   Washington, D.C. 20530

UNITED STATES SENATOR

SALUTATION: Dear Senator Collins,
CLOSING: Sincerely yours,
INVITATION, MAN: Senator Stephen Collins or
　　　　　　　　　Mr. and Mrs. Stephen Collins
　　　　WOMAN: Senator Margaret Collins or
　　　　　　　　　Mr. and Mrs. Stephen Collins
SOCIAL ENVELOPE, MAN: The Honorable Stephen Collins
　　　　　　　　　and Mrs. Collins
　　　　WOMAN: The Honorable Margaret Collins
　　　　　　　　　and Mr. Collins
OFFICIAL ENVELOPE: The Honorable Margaret Collins
　　　　　　　　　United States Senate
　　　　　　　　　Washington, D.C. 20510

THE SPEAKER OF THE HOUSE OF REPRESENTATIVES

SALUTATION: Dear Mr. (Madam) Speaker,
CLOSING: Sincerely yours,
INVITATION, MAN: The Speaker of the House and Mrs. Barscz or
　　　　　　　　　The Speaker and Mrs. Barscz
　　　　WOMAN: The Speaker of the House and Mr. Barscz or
　　　　　　　　　The Speaker and Mr. Barscz
SOCIAL ENVELOPE, MAN: The Speaker of the House and Mrs. Barscz
　　　　WOMAN: The Speaker of the House and Mr. Barscz
OFFICIAL ENVELOPE: The Honorable Joyce Barscz
　　　　　　　　　Speaker of the House of Representatives
　　　　　　　　　The Capitol
　　　　　　　　　Washington, D.C. 20515

MEMBER OF THE HOUSE OF REPRESENTATIVES

SALUTATION: Dear Mr. (Mrs.) Covington,
CLOSING: Sincerely yours,
INVITATION: Mr. and Mrs. Samuel Covington
SOCIAL ENVELOPE, MAN: The Honorable Samuel Covington
                                        and Mrs. Covington
                    WOMAN: The Honorable Jean Covington
                                        and Mr. Covington
OFFICIAL ENVELOPE: The Honorable Samuel Covington
                                House of Representatives
                                Washington, D.C. 20515

THE CHIEF JUSTICE OF THE SUPREME COURT

SALUTATION: Dear Mr. (Madam) Chief Justice,
CLOSING: Sincerely yours,
INVITATION, MAN: The Chief Justice and Mrs. Holmes
                WOMAN: The Chief Justice and Mr. Holmes
SOCIAL ENVELOPE, MAN: The Chief Justice and Mrs. Holmes
                        Woman: The Chief Justice and Mr. Holmes
OFFICIAL ENVELOPE: The Chief Justice of The Supreme Court
                                Washington, D.C. 20543

ASSOCIATE JUSTICE OF THE SUPREME COURT

SALUTATION: Dear Mr. (Madam) Justice,
CLOSING: Sincerely yours,
INVITATION, MAN: Mr. Justice Gladstone and Mrs. Gladstone
                WOMAN: Madam Justice Cladstone and Mr. Cladstone
SOCIAL ENVELOPE, MAN: Mr. Justice Gladstone and Mrs. Gladstone
                        WOMAN: Madam Justice Gladstone and Mr. Gladstone
Official Envelope: Mr. (Madam) Justice Gladstone
                                The Supreme Court
                                Washington, D.C. 20543

UNITED STATES AMBASSADOR TO THE UNITED NATIONS

SALUTATION: Dear Mr. (Madam) Ambassador,

CLOSING: Sincerely yours,

INVITATION: Mr. and Mrs. Donald Eisemann

SOCIAL ENVELOPE, MAN: The United States Representative to the
United Nations and Mrs. Eisemann

WOMAN: The United States Representative to the
United Nations and Mr. Eisemann

OFFICIAL ENVELOPE: The Honorable Donald Eisemann
The United States Representative
to The United Nations
United Nations Plaza
New York, NY 10017

AMERICAN AMBASSADOR

SALUTATION: Dear Mr. (Madam) Ambassador,

CLOSING: Sincerely yours,

INVITATION: Mr. and Mrs. Harold Dickey

SOCIAL ENVELOPE, MAN: The Ambassador of the United States
and Mrs. Dickey

WOMAN: The Ambassador of the United States
and Mr. Dickey

OFFICIAL ENVELOPE: The Honorable Harold Dickey
The Ambassador of the United States
Tokyo, Japan

SECRETARY GENERAL OF THE UNITED NATIONS

SALUTATION: Dear Mr. (Madam) Secretary General,
CLOSING: Sincerely yours,
INVITATION, MAN: The Secretary General of the United
                  Nations and Mrs. Venezia
        WOMAN: The Secretary General of the United
                  Nations and Mr. Venezia
SOCIAL ENVELOPE, MAN: His Excellency, The Secretary General
                        of the United Nations and Mrs. Venezia
              WOMAN: Her Excellency, The Secretary
                        General of the United Nations and Mr. Venezia
OFFICIAL ENVELOPE: His (Her) Excellency,
                    The Secretary General of the United Nations
                    United Nations Plaza
                    New York, NY 10017

FOREIGN AMBASSADOR

SALUTATION: Dear Mr. (Madam) Ambassador.
CLOSING: Sincerely yours,
INVITATION, MAN: The Ambassador of Spain and Mrs. Orlando
        WOMAN: The Ambassador of Spain and Mr. Orlando
SOCIAL ENVELOPE, MAN: His Excellency, The Ambassador of
                        Spain and Mrs. Orlando
              WOMAN: Her Excellency, The Ambassador of
                        Spain and Mr. Orlando
OFFICIAL ENVELOPE: His (Her) Excellency Juan Orlando
                    Ambassador of Spain

GOVERNOR

SALUTATION: Dear Governor Clinton,
CLOSING: Sincerely yours,
INVITATION, MAN: The Governor of New York and Mrs. Clinton
        WOMAN: The Governor of New York and Mr. Clinton
SOCIAL ENVELOPE, MAN: The Governor and Mrs. Clinton
              WOMAN: The Governor and Mr. Clinton
OFFICIAL ENVELOPE: The Honorable George Clinton
                    Governor of New York

STATE SENATOR OR REPRESENTATIVE

SALUTATION: Dear Mr. (Mrs) Flanagan,

CLOSING: Sincerely yours,

INVITATION: Mr. and Mrs. John Flanagan

SOCIAL ENVELOPE, MAN: The Honorable John Flanagan
and Mrs. Flanagan

          WOMAN: The Honorable Mary Flanagan
and Mr. Flanagan

OFFICIAL ENVELOPE: The Honorable John Flanagan

MAYOR

SALUTATION: Dear Mayor Santiago,

CLOSING: Sincerely yours,

INVITATION, MAN: The Mayor of Santa Fe and Mrs. Santiago

       WOMAN: The Mayor of Sante Fe and Mr. Santiago

SOCIAL ENVELOPE, MAN: The Honorable Paul Santiago
and Mrs. Santiago

          WOMAN: The Honorable Carla Santiago
and Mr. Santiago

OFFICIAL ENVELOPE: The Honorable Carla Santiago

JUDGE

SALUTATION: Dear Judge Knapp,

CLOSING: Sincerely yours,

INVITATION, MAN: Judge and Mrs. Harold Knapp

       WOMAN: Mr. and Mrs. Harold Knapp

BOTH ARE JUDGES: The Judges Knapp

THE POPE

SALUTATION: Your Holiness, or Most Holy Father,

CLOSING: Your Most humble servant,

ENVELOPE: His Holiness Pope John Paul II

CARDINAL

SALUTATION: Your Eminence, or Dear Cardinal McGrath
CLOSING: Your humble servant,
ENVELOPE: His Eminence, John Cardinal McGrath

ARCHBISHOP

SALUTATION: Your Excellency, or Dear Archbishop Daley,
CLOSING: Your obedient servant,
ENVELOPE: The Most Reverend Francis Xavier Daley

BISHOP

SALUTATION: Most Reverend Sir, or Dear Bishop Carlucci,
CLOSING: Your obedient servant,
Envelope: The Most Reverend Peter Carlucci

ABBOT

SALUTATION: Right Reverend Johnson, or Dear Father Johnson,
CLOSING: Your obedient servant,
ENVELOPE: The Right Reverend Laurence Johnson

MONSIGNOR

SALUTATION: Right Reverend Monsignor, or Dear Monsignor LaRue,
CLOSING: Yours faithfully,
ENVELOPE: The Right Reverend Monsignor Stephen LaRue

PRIEST

SALUTATION: Reverend Father, or Dear Father O'Malley,
CLOSING: Yours faithfully,
ENVELOPE: The Reverend Father Patrick O'Malley

BROTHER

SALUTATION: Dear Brother Andrew,
CLOSING: Yours faithfully,
ENVELOPE: Brother Andrew, (initials of his order)

MOTHER SUPERIOR

SALUTATION: Dear Reverend Mother,
CLOSING: Yours faithfully,
ENVELOPE: The Reverend Mother Emily

SISTER

SALUTATION: Dear Sister Mary,
CLOSING: Yours faithfully,
ENVELOPE: Sister Mary, (initials of his order)

EPISCOPAL BISHOP

SALUTATION: Right Reverend Sir, or Dear Bishop,
CLOSING: Sincerely yours,
SOCIAL ENVELOPE: The Right Reverend and Mrs. Leland Osgood
OFFICIAL ENVELOPE: The Right Reverend Leland Osgood, D.D.
Bishop of Philadelphia

PROTESTANT CLERGY

SALUTATION: Dear Mr. (Mrs.) Stapleton,
CLOSING: Sincerely yours,
INVITATION, MAN: The Reverend And Mrs. James Stapleton
Woman: Mr. and Mrs. James Stapleton
SOCIAL ENVELOPE, MAN: The Reverend and Mrs. James Stapleton
WOMAN: Mr. and Mrs. James Stapleton
OFFICIAL ENVELOPE: The Reverend Lucille Stapleton

PROTESTANT CLERGY WITH DOCTORATE

SALUTATION: Dear Dr. Kingston,
CLOSING: Sincerely yours,
INVITATION, MAN: The Reverend Dr. and Mrs. Frederic Kingston
WOMAN: Mr. and Mrs. Frederic Kingston
SOCIAL ENVELOPE, MAN: The Reverend Dr. and Mrs. Frederic Kingston
WOMAN: Mr. and Mrs. Frederic Kingston
OFFICIAL ENVELOPE: The Reverend Dr. Linda Kingston

RABBI

SALUTATION: Dear Rabbi Levine,
CLOSING: Sincerely yours,
INVITATION: Rabbi and Mrs. Daniel Levine
SOCIAL ENVELOPE: Rabbi And Mrs. Daniel Levine
OFFICIAL ENVELOPE: Rabbi Daniel Levine

RABBI WITH DOCTORATE

SALUTATION: Dear Rabbi Feldman, or Dear Dr. Feldman,
CLOSING: Sincerely yours,
INVITATION: Rabbi and Mrs. Stanley Feldman or
              (Dr.) and Mrs. Stanley Feldman
SOCIAL ENVELOPE: Rabbi (Dr.) and Mrs. Stanley Feldman
OFFICIAL ENVELOPE: Rabbi Stanley Feldman

ABOUT
CRANE AND
CO., INC.

*I*n 1776, the Massachusetts Bay Colony issued the first colonial bank notes that were backed by a colony and not by the English Crown. Stephen Crane's mill produced the paper for those bank notes and sold them to Paul Revere. Although better known for his midnight ride, Paul Revere engraved those first colonial bank notes.

In 1799, Stephen's son, Zenas Crane, headed west to search for a site for a mill of his own. He needed a place with an abundant supply of fresh water (for power and for cleansing the rags used in papermaking) and where the surrounding area would produce both an ample supply of rags for use as a raw material and a growing market. (Housewives saved their rags and sold them or bartered them to the general store. A rag merchant bought the rags and resold them to the paper mill, where they were transformed into paper.)

Zenas Crane's search ended in Dalton, Massachusetts, a small agricultural community nestled in the Berkshire Hills. Dalton's location gave him the water he needed and access to southern markets through New York City and western markets through Albany, New York.

In partnership with John Willard and Henry Wiswall, Zenas Crane purchased a fourteen-acre site for the sum of $194. Crane & Co., Inc. was founded in 1801 when the new company placed an advertisement in the *Pittsfield*

Sun asking ladies to sell them their rags.

Zenas Crane's company produced paper for businesses, printers, and publishers. He also sold paper to the independent banks that were authorized to print paper money.

Bond paper is a paper with a hard finish that is used for bonds, stock certificates, and business letterheads. The term was first used in 1850 when the president of a New York bank wrote to Crane asking for some "bond paper." The term soon became the generic term for the type of paper used for bonds.

Also at that time, paper money was being counterfeited by a process called raising the money, which was the illegal process of changing, for example, a one dollar bill into a ten dollar bill, by drawing a zero after the one on the bill. In 1844, Crane developed a technique to put silk threads in its bank-note paper to prevent the raising of money. Crane put a single thread in one dollar bills, two threads in two dollar bills, and three threads in three dollar bills. If somebody held what appeared to be a ten dollar bill to the light and saw a single silk thread, he knew that the bill was counterfeit.

Crane's mastering of this innovative technique was instrumental in the company's landing a contract in 1879 to supply the paper for the currency of the United States. Since that day, Crane has supplied virtually all U.S. currency paper to the United States Bureau of Engraving and Printing. Crane also supplies currency and bank-note paper to the governments of some forty other countries.

The company Zenas Crane founded in 1801 has grown, prospered, and diversified but is still owned by his descendants, still makes 100-percent cotton fiber papers, and still adheres to the quality standards on which he insisted.

Crane products today include currency and security papers, ledger and record papers, architectural and engineering drafting papers, nonwoven technical products, and a complete line of business and social stationery papers for corporate letterheads, social correspondence, and wedding invitations.

INDEX

INDEX

INDEX

INDEX

INDEX

INDEX

INDEX

INDEX

INDEX

INDEX

INDEX

INDEX

INDEX

INDEX

150

INDEX